A Hall of Fame Book

FOOTBALL

by John Mosedale

WORLD PUBLISHING
TIMES MIRROR
NEW YORK

To Andy and Mike
And the boys of The Alexander Robertson School
New York City

All photographs in this book are courtesy of the Pro
Football Hall of Fame, Canton, Ohio. Special thanks
are due Don Smith, Director of Public Relations for the
Pro Football Hall of Fame, and Pat Berry, Librarian
of the Pro Football Hall of Fame.
The Babe Dimancheff anecdote on pages 37-38 comes from
"How to Take a Biscuit Apart and Put it Together"
by Gerald Holland in *Sports Illustrated,*
September 18, 1961. Copyright 1961 by Time, Inc.

Published by The World Publishing Company
110 East 59th Street, New York, N.Y. 10022
Published simultaneously in Canada by
Nelson, Foster & Scott Ltd.

WORLD PUBLISHING
TIMES MIRROR

CONTENTS

PREFACE

On a summery September seventeenth in 1920, 11 men met in the Ralph Hays Hupmobile Agency in Canton, Ohio, an industrial town some 67 miles south of Cleveland. The Hupmobile no longer exists, having gone the way of the Willys, the Essex, the Edsel and the dinosaur. But that session changed the face of professional sport in America. Out of it emerged the American Professional Football League, which two years later became the National Football League, now governing for more than 50 years the most violent and thrilling of team sports.

To be sure, professional football players existed before the meeting. The first, according to the best evidence, was the wonderfully-named W. W. "Pudge" Hefflefinger, in 1888 a Yale All-American as celebrated as Johnny Unitas or "Broadway" Joe Namath today.

The evidence is a receipt noting he played in a game between two Pittsburgh athletic clubs in 1892 for $500 in addition to furnishing three players from Chicago for "twice train fare." His salary was out of line: the University of Michigan All-American Willie Heston tried to auction himself to the highest bidder upon graduating in 1905 and found no takers.

A standard of ten dollars per man was set in what is held to be the first game in which all the players were paid—Pennsylvania's Latrobe versus Jeannette, September 3, 1895. Top wage of $25 went to the Latrobe quarterback, a busy lad named John K. Brailer, who simultaneously starred for Indiana High School and Indiana Normal College in Pennsylvania before going on to a respectable career in dentistry.

The following year Brailer brought his West Virginia teammates to play for Latrobe at a going rate of $150 for a half-season. There were no schedules yet, games being arranged on a week-to-week basis. Players were often college men working under assumed names, offering their Sunday services to the highest bidder following a Saturday of toiling for alma mater. In 1915 for instance, Knute Rockne faced the Columbus Panhandles six times, each time representing a different team.

Payments, scheduling and rules were rudimentary. The roughneck game bore less resemblance to the pro-set T-formation game of today than it did to rugby, the sport from which American football had emerged only recently.

The common ancestor, to backtrack a bit, is soccer, which the rest of the world calls "football"—a free-flowing game of 11 men who roam the field, attempting to kick a ball into a net guarded by a goalie. Its basic restriction is that a player cannot handle the ball.

At Rugby, England, there is a plaque to William Webb Ellis, who in 1823 "with a fine disregard for the rules of the game, first took the ball in his arms and ran with it." That game, named after its place of origin, shortly emigrated to American shores.

Rugby evolved into American football, first played by colleges when Princeton met Rutgers in 1869. This was a rough, brutal game in which players massed about the ball at scrum, charging at each other until the weaker team flagged. The emphasis was on violence and oxlike strength. So frequent and severe were the injuries that the forward pass was legislated into existence decades later to open up the sport and reduce the bloodletting before legislators closed it down.

During the early years of the twentieth century, in a nation largely given over to a love of baseball, the sport prospered to a point where professional or semi-professional town teams flourished, if only briefly. It was particularly received well in the coal and steel communities of New York, Pennsylvania and Ohio, where hard-nosed workers found it good recreation as spectator or player.

So, to bring some order to the chaotic scheduling and staffing of teams the 11 men conspired in the Hays agency. Rivalries already existed and had been broken off between such communities as Canton and Massillon. The men hoped to capitalize on a growing enthusiasm for the sport, which by that time had produced such college stars as Walter Camp, Jim Thorpe and

Knute Rockne; such great rivalries as Harvard-Yale and Army-Navy; and such great teams as Fielding Yost's "point-a-minute" University of Michigan team, which one year scored 600 points, allowing the opposition 13.

It was one of Yost's great rivals, Coach Robert Zuppke of Illinois, who said at a 1917 commencement banquet, "Why do I always lose my football players just when they have begun to play the game?" Among his auditors was a young Illinois end named George Halas.

Halas was one of the men meeting in the auto agency on behalf of the Decatur Staleys. There were also representatives of the Chicago Cardinals; the Dayton Triangles; the Cleveland Indians; the Massillon Tigers; the Canton Bulldogs; teams from Muncie and Hammond, Indiana; Rochester, New York; and Rock Island, Illinois.

The local newspaper reported the meeting in only five paragraphs, including the news that the first president of the new league would be the world's greatest athlete, Jim Thorpe, chosen by Canton to re-establish its football team, disbanded ten years earlier following charges of a fix against Massillon.

Most of the charter cities shortly dropped out, giving way to larger communities able to support the game as its popularity grew. Thirty years later, some 40 cities had come and gone in the National Football League, with the Chicago Bears (formerly the Staleys), the St. Louis (formerly Chicago) Cardinals and the Green Bay Packers laying claim to the longest unbroken memberships.

The game itself changed beyond the vision of the canniest of those present. None of them could foresee an era when a medium called television would record the deeds of a Roger Staubach, or whisk viewers in prairie farms and city apartments to Super Bowls where 90,000 watched athletes half again the size of the ruggedest player of the twenties twist through formations not yet perfected. Franchises which in 1920 went for $100 would cost millions by 1972. But "oddly enough," a commentator noted, "the latter price is the best buy."

No memorial plaque, like that to young Ellis, marks the spot. of that September meeting, now a U.S. post office. But just blocks away there is a monument of Indiana limestone, a $750,000

Since its completion in 1963, more than 800,000 people have passed through the portals of the Pro Football Hall of Fame in Canton, Ohio.

museum with a football-shaped dome. Beyond its half-ton, heroic copper statue of three players, more than 12,000 photographs, 2,000 books, two miles of film, muddied shoes, bloodied jerseys and 5,000 programs of contests forgotten by many participants chronicle the growth of this great game.

For here memory speaks of tall deeds and improbable events; of gore, glory and excitement unsurpassed in sport; of heroes with feet of mercury and of clay; of the immortal, the great and the merely plucky who seized on a moment, recalling an era when there seemed giants in the earth and eagles in the air. Possibly they were only players of a boys' game up against a greater world of war and depression. Yet they have grown great by deeds, however varied in size and accomplishment, immortalized by achievement in the Professional Football Hall of Fame.

THORPE!

t is appropriate that the first figure in the Hall of Fame, standing inside the front door, is a bronze statue of Jim Thorpe, quite simply the greatest athlete this nation ever produced.

Thorpe, as noted, was first president of the league organized by the men in Ralph Hays' showroom. But more importantly, he was the most famous athlete of his time, the Canton Bulldog star whose fame and feats steadied the shaky league and helped establish football in the midwestern heartland.

At seven feet the statue is somewhat larger than life-size, but at six feet one inch and 190 pounds, so was Thorpe. It is said of some men that they are legends in their own time. Strictly speaking, a legend is fiction; the Thorpe legend was largely true.

Playing for the tiny U.S. Indian Industrial School at Carlisle, Pennsylvania, he scored 198 points in 1911, as the Indians defeated the champions of the East, Midwest and Pacific Coast. Against mighty Harvard, then a football giant, his legs encased in bandages because of injuries, Thorpe scored a touchdown and drop-kicked four field goals in an astonishing 18-15 upset. The next year he ran back a kickoff 95 yards for a touchdown against Army; a penalty against Carlisle nullified the score, so Army kicked off again. Thorpe ran that one back 105 yards for a touch-

down. A cadet attempting to tackle him in that game was injured in such a way that he never played football again, but
Dwight D. Eisenhower never forgot Jim Thorpe and the 27-6
loss he handed Army.

In 1913 Thorpe went to Stockholm with the U.S. Olympic
team. He won both the pentathlon and decathlon events. The
pentathlon aims at testing an athlete's versatility, measuring his
accomplishments in the 100-yard dash, long jump, shot put, high
jump, 400-meter run, 100-meter high hurdles, discus, pole vault,
javelin and 1,500-meter run. Although he had never seen a javelin before and pretty much trained for the competition in a
hammock, Thorpe not only broke records for the event, but
came close to equaling world records for some of the specialties
involved.

Small wonder that Sweden's King Gustav V, presenting him
with medals, said, "You, sir, are the greatest athlete in the world."

Said Thorpe, "Thanks, King."

There was little that Thorpe could not do in athletics. He shot
golf in the seventies. He played major league baseball for seven
seasons with the New York Giants, Cincinnati Reds and Boston
Braves. The saying was that he showed a weakness for the high-
ball off the field and the curve ball on, but Thorpe, pointing to
his final season batting average of .329 with Boston, said, "I must
have hit a few curves."

Off the field the story was less a triumph. He drank. He was
irresponsible and fell on hard times. He said, "sometimes I think
I might have done better in some other line . . . than the athletic
business." He worked variously as a bit player in the movies, a
ditch digger, a plant guard for the Ford Motor Company, a
saloon host, a wrestling manager, a lecturer and a merchant
sailor—anything to earn money. Coupled with the shameful re-
scinding of his medals by the Olympic committee, this led many
to speak of "the tragedy of Jim Thorpe" and to view his life as a
sorry story. But, apart from wanting his trophies back, Thorpe
never complained, and one of his sons said he was "a happy-go-
lucky man who would give you the shirt off his back."

There are those who find sadness in a sunrise; for all the "poor
Indian" stories about Thorpe, he was named by the widest margin "athlete of the half-century" in a coast-to-coast poll by the

Associated Press, decades after he had played his last game.

Thorpe was born in a one-room log cabin in Prague, near Shawnee, Oklahoma, May 28, 1888. His father's father was an Irishman who married a granddaughter of the famous Sac and Fox warrior, Chief Blackhawk, for whom the Blackhawk Wars of 1831 were named. Thorpe's Indian mother christened him Wa-Tho-Huck, or Bright Path.

As a boy Thorpe wandered the fields, raced rabbits, hunted, fished, and chased — some say wrestled — bears and avoided school. He was sent to Carlisle, a vocational school, as an apprentice tailor. In the free and easy manner of the day, his athletic career at Carlisle spanned the years 1907-1912, including seasons when he dropped out.

Football had only recently been introduced to Carlisle by a former Yale quarterback. The Indians did not immediately understand the white man's strangest and most complicated sport, then characterized by the president of Columbia University as, "not one of those games decently played by decent young men."

But Carlisle had acquired its first full-time coach, Glenn S. "Pop" Warner, a young Cornell graduate who quit law to coach the game he loved, inventing along the way the single- and double-wing formations and the cross body block.

It was not only Army and Harvard that Carlisle humiliated. Breaking up a scoreless tie against Brown, Thorpe faked a punt and ran through the entire team from his end zone. "Do you think that fellow Thorpe is human?" a Brown player asked after the game. "If I hit that Indian once today, I hit him a thousand times, and I haven't got him yet."

Thorpe, like his classmates, believed he could vindicate his race in football where the struggle was even. "You outnumbered us, and you also had the press agents," a young Sioux told Warner. "When the white man won, it was always a battle. When we won, it was a massacre."

The Indians, playing the biggest and best football teams of their day, never averaged more than 170 pounds or carried more than two or three substitutes.

"Here were three hard, bruising struggles all in a row," wrote Warner, "yet on the following Saturday we traveled to Cambridge for a game with Harvard. Percy Haughton started with

Jim Thorpe was voted the greatest athlete of the half-century. The Thorpe statue dominates the Hall of Fame, and annually a trophy in his name goes to the game's outstanding player.

his second team, which was just about as good as the first, and late in the second half when every Carlisle man was out on his feet, sent in his regulars, all fresh and rampant.

"When I hear people say that Indians can't stand the gaff, I always think of that finish against Harvard. Jim Thorpe, bandaged from head to foot, kicked four field goals, one from the 48-yard line, and his battered, crippled mates, in as fine an exhibition of sheer grit as I have ever seen, not only beat back the rushes of fresh men but swept them down the field, winning by a score of 18 to 15."

Following the custom of college athletes then, Thorpe picked up money by playing semi-professional baseball in the summer. Unlike many, he did not bother to play under an assumed name. After his Olympic triumphs his play-for-pay career was revealed by a newspaper. The Olympic committee struck his records from the books and confiscated not only his medals but a jewel-encrusted Viking ship presented to him by Czar Nicholas II of Russia and a bust from King Gustav.

Although he had done no more than many other athletes, Thorpe understood he had violated the amateur code. But to the end of his life, he protested bitterly the loss of the awards from the king and the czar, which he regarded as private gifts. They were never returned.

During all the publicity over the recall of the medals, Thorpe signed with the New York baseball Giants, one of many clubs that sought him. He never lived up to his promise as a major league player, attributing this to the fact that he never played regularly, 77 games with Cincinnati being his top for a single season.

Perhaps this was partly because he quickly ran afoul of the Giants' manager, the feisty, immortal John McGraw, "Little Napoleon," as he was called. McGraw disliked college athletes. Thorpe compounded the problem by wrenching the arm of a star pitcher in a friendly wrestling contest. Thereafter he was under orders not to touch a teammate, which was probably just as well, considering his strength and agility.

In 1915 Thorpe helped organize the rebirth of a team in Canton, "the cradle of professional football," combining it with baseball as an off-season activity. This was five years before the American Professional Football League was organized with Thorpe serving as token president because of his great fame. The vital role he played in those early years popularizing the sport in the Middle West was characterized by George Halas, who called Thorpe "the man who made our game possible."

McGraw disapproved of Thorpe's autumnal activity, suggesting "Old Jim," as he called himself, quit the game. Thorpe asked why.

"You might get hurt," McGraw suggested.

"How can anyone get hurt playing football?" asked Thorpe.

He knew better, of course.

The records of those early years are as sketchy as Thorpe's training habits, but he recalled once punting 90 yards for Canton and kicking a 75-yard field goal against Indianapolis, and that's something you never saw on television.

"He had a way of running I never saw before," a teammate said. "We didn't wear helmets much in those days. Jim would shift his hip toward the guy about to tackle him, then swing it away and then, when the player moved in to hit him, he'd swing his hip back hard against the player's head and leave him lying there."

Just how good Thorpe was is best understood in stories told by some of football's outstanding figures who remembered their experiences against him. Knute Rockne, who went on to revolutionize football as the greatest coach of his day at Notre Dame, played against Thorpe as left end for the archenemy Massillon Tigers. Rockne felt every reason to be confident of his own ability. He was fresh from college where he and teammate Gus Dorais made Notre Dame a recognized football power and popularized the forward pass in a stunning upset against Army.

And so, on an early play from scrimmage, he spilled Thorpe for a loss.

"You shouldn't do that, Rock," Thorpe remonstrated. "The people came to see Old Jim run. Be a good boy and let him run."

Rockne dropped Thorpe again.

"I told you, Rock," said Thorpe, "these people came to see Old Jim run. You better let him run."

Rockne dug in again. He was prepared to put the wood to Thorpe all game long, wondering meanwhile if the stories about Thorpe's greatness were exaggerated.

There was the explosion of leather smiting leather. Lying dazed on the ground, Rockne heard the crowd break into cheers as Thorpe ran 60 yards for a touchdown. A strong hand pulled him to his feet and he looked into the friendly face of Thorpe.

"That's the way to do it," said Thorpe. "You let Old Jim run."

Decades later, Jim Brown of the Cleveland Browns, who was the greatest ground-gainer in NFL history, would limp back to the huddle slowly, groaning and sighing after being tackled. Watching him, you would doubt that he could stay in the game;

certainly it would be a couple of plays before he could be trusted to carry the ball. And then on the very next play he would blast the line. Or a great receiver like Paul Warfield of the Miami Dolphins loafs through his pass patterns until the defender relaxes or takes his eye off him, then he flares into full speed. Football requires great concentration; the worst injuries and greatest gains are chalked up when a player lets down.

George Halas, one of the men in the auto showroom who was present at the creation of the league, began his pro career playing for the Decatur Staleys. He would take them to Chicago, where they became the mighty Bears, and as player, coach and owner, Halas would be the only man active in professional football from its founding to the present day. He literally has seen every great player of the game. And he has his memories of Thorpe, one of them still in the record book.

Halas once caught a pass near the goal line, stumbled and crawled on. In the early days a player was allowed to get up and run after being tackled, but the rule was changed because of the frequent injuries in just such a situation as this.

"It was a foolish thing to do," Halas recalled, "because I had every right to expect two knees in the small of my back. But the guy who hit me was the big Indian. His legs straddled me.

"'All right, Georgie,'" he said, "'If you want to play at being a horse, I'll ride you.' And he rode my nose right into the dirt."

Those two men wrote a play into the record books on November 8, 1928 when Halas recovered a Thorpe fumble on the two-yard line. He ran 98 yards for a touchdown with Old Jim in pursuit, at least partly inspired by the fear of what Thorpe would do to him if he got his hands on him. That Halas dash understandably remains the longest run with a recovered fumble.

"Thorpe was a great defensive player, too," Halas pointed out. "His tackling was as unusual as his running style—he never tackled with his arms and shoulders. He'd leg-whip the ball carrier. If he hit you from behind, he'd throw that big body across your back and nearly break you in two." One of those tackles finished Dorais, Rockne's former Notre Dame teammate, as a player.

Thorpe's Carlise coach, Pop Warner, went on to the West Coast, where he coached great Stanford teams. It is a measure

of Warner's contributions to the game that the Pop Warner
Leagues, named for him, offer some boys their first chances to
play organized football. At Stanford, Warner coached Ernie
Nevers, who once single-handedly gained more yards than the
entire opposing backfield against Notre Dame's famed "Four
Horseman." Warner unhesitatingly picked Nevers over Thorpe
as the greatest player he ever coached because the big, shock-
haired Californian gave 100 percent of himself on every play,
while Thorpe sometimes played only as hard as he felt.

But Nevers remembers it otherwise. After college he starred
for the Duluth Eskimos. To give you an idea of how differently
the sport was played in those days, the Eskimos once left home
in early September and returned in January after playing 29
games (the present regular season is 14 games, and its outcome
is partly decided by which team has the fewest injured players)
and traveling 19,000 miles. They played five games in one eight-
day stretch. Nevers missed only 27 minutes of 1,740 played, and
remember that players went both ways at that time, on both
offense and defense.

He was only 23 and fresh out of college when he played
against Thorpe, who was 38 and two years away from his final
game with Akron.

As Ernie reached for a pass, Thorpe belted him. "Never, before or since," said Nevers, "have I been tackled so hard." That
hard tackling gave rise to the story that Thorpe slipped sheets
of galvanized iron between layers of his shoulder pads. But they
were sole leather, made to specification by a Canton shoemaker,
until the league outlawed them. The warning remained, "Never
turn your back to Old Jim on a pass."

Thorpe played for 16 years. He left Canton after rumors of a
betting coup in which he allegedly encouraged talk that he was
too injured to play, then suited up for a romp over Massillon. His
brief tenure as league commissioner was unsatisfactory. He
could not control himself, let alone an organization. The crowds
grew and so did the responsibilities. Through lean financial days
as the league struggled to establish itself, leadership of a greater
quality than Thorp's was required. But in the early days his
shining reputation carried the league when it faltered.

His life wound down into a skein of odd jobs. His name popped

The Canton Bulldogs, typical of the steel and rubber town teams early in the century, were charter members of the organization that became the National Football League.

up from time to time in the reminiscence of some who recalled "the greatest athlete of all time" in action. He agitated for the return of his trophies and involved himself sporadically on behalf of his tribe's rights, at a time when Indians were conventionally more callously regarded than now. Perhaps in this day of greater concern over the mistreatment of the Indians, Thorpe's story might have ended on a brighter note.

He died of a heart attack in a Los Angeles suburb. Typically, following his stormy life, there was argument over his burial ground. First he lay near his birthplace, where a great tomb was to be erected. When his third wife moved his body to Tulsa after a couple of years, that project foundered.

He was buried again in a $17,000 pink mausoleum in the Pennsylvania community of Mauch Chunk, which in a referendum changed its name to Jim Thorpe, an effort by the citizens to attract attention and hopefully, new industry.

"All we got," said the mayor bitterly, "was a new name and a dead Indian."

But his name lives on more proudly. The Jim Thorpe Memorial Trophy is presented each year to the outstanding player in the NFL. It is one trophy they can never take away from him.

2 / CORRIDOR OF COLOSSALS

Behind the statue of Thorpe, a curving ramp ascends to the exhibition rotunda. Pillars along the ramp offer photographs of the men who oversaw the development of professional football from a haphazard group of rough-and-readies to the sport voted most popular in the United States.

There are Joseph E. Carr, founder of the Columbus Panhandles, who succeeded Thorpe as president when the league was still in its thumb-sucking stage, serving from 1921 to 1939; and Carl Storck, president for the following two years.

Then the club owners named the league's first commissioner— Elmer Layden, "the Thin Man" of Notre Dame, fullback on the most famous of all college backfields, Knute Rockne's Four Horsemen.

Layden became commissioner after seven years as athletic director and head football coach at his alma mater, thus adding glamour to the league as a major league operation.

He served five tough years as commissioner. The league met opposition from the All-American Football Conference, whose offers of interleague competition were answered with an unfortunate crack of Layden's, "... get a football." World War II mounted a major strain on the sport's resources.

When Layden resigned under some pressure in 1946, he was succeeded by a compromise choice, Bert Bell, co-owner of the Philadelphia Eagles. It was a happy act of fate.

Bell came from a respected Philadelphia mainline family with an ancestral background of politics and high society. But he found he couldn't give up football after playing at the University of Pennsylvania. He coached there, and in the early 1930s bought the Philadelphia Eagles.

In addition to coaching the team, he peddled tickets—often standing on streetcorners and offering them to passers-by. The story goes that one day he found more reporters in the press box on game day than there were customers in the stands.

But as commissioner he proved tougher than any of the owners, whose interests often set them to wrangling with each other. And he devised the program which more than any other single factor lifted pro football to major league status—televising road games and blacking out home contests within a 72-mile radius of the stadium. This introduced customers to the excitement of the great game and made them pay for the privilege of watching at home.

Television was a new medium and Bell's handling of the problem stands as one of the far-reaching decisions in sport. In contrast, baseball allowed each club owner to do as he would, including televising of all games, and learned anew the reluctance of the human animal to pay for what he can get free.

Another major Bell innovation aimed at keeping play even was to implement the draft, giving the poorest team rights to the best college players and so equalizing the competition that he liked to say, "On any given Sunday, any team can beat any other team in the NFL."

Attendance soared. There could be no doubt now about its future. And one sunny day in 1959, "Death came for him at a game between the Philadelphia Eagles and the Pittsburgh Steelers . . . and the stands were full, which must have made him very happy. As much as any one man, he was responsible for the filled stands.

"He died at a professional football game," wrote Tex Maule in The Pros, "and I guess if you had asked Bert Bell the way he wanted to go, he would have said, 'At a pro football game.'"

Bell's successor was another compromise choice, Alvin "Pete" Rozelle, former general manager for the Los Angeles Rams. And again the fates were generous. Rozelle is generally regarded as the outstanding commissioner in all sports. *Sports Illustrated* magazine tapped him, a non-athlete, as its "Sportsman of the Year." Under his leadership the NFL increased from 12 to 26 teams; the war between the league and the American Football Conference was settled equitably. Television revenues jumped to $43,000,000 a year and compared to other elements in American life, football charted its course smoothly through years of unrest.

It is like being passenger on a space capsule through time, stepping from the ramp and its reminder of television, Super Bowls and crowds of 80,000 to the exhibition rotunda, where the first exhibit along the wall is called, "The Birthplace—the Cradle" and reminds you that "pro football was forged in steel and coal towns. At first, sturdy mill and mining lads played for the sheer joy of combat, but one fine day...."

Here old programs, tattered newspaper columns and photographs, aging helmets, leather noseguards and curiously round footballs reflect the age of Hefflefinger and Brailer and teams like the Youngstown Patricians, Staats AC, Wheeling, West Virginia, the Portsmouth Spartans and Rochester Jeffs.

Elsewhere an exhibit recounts the emergence of the Patricians Club of St. Patrick's Church, Youngstown, Ohio, into "the champions of Mahoning County, 1914" and "1915 World Champion" after the importing of college stars. Half time entertainment was a barbershop quartet.

Prehistory becomes recorded deed with a photo of "Thorpe of Carlisle," a parkaed figure in crimson "taking a breather on the bench" behind an official program of athletic awards at Carlisle, January 31, 1912.

A program advertises Charley Brickley (late of Harvard) and "his den of Tigers versus Thorpe and his cage of Bulldogs" at Myers Lake Park, Canton, November 25, 1917 in "the first game for world championship"— surely an empty boast. Admission: one dollar.

"Canton Bulldogs Wrest Victory from Tigers," a headline informs us. "Two Massillon Fumbles Converted into Points for

Great Victory"—and we stand at a dawn of history, for on the professional level and on to the present day with high-powered high school teams, the Ohio communities of Canton and Massillon predate any contemporary rivalries—yes, even Green Bay and Chicago—and match them in enthusiasm and bloodletting.

Three early Massillon players who achieved fame as college participants were Gus Dorais, who threw those passes to Rockne; Jock Sutherland, coach of the great University of Pittsburgh teams of the 1930s and the Steelers in the 1940s, who stuck stubbornly to the single wing; and Claude "Tiny" Thornhill, who took Stanford to the Rose Bowl.

The climb into sport respectability is outlined amid the next collection of memorabilia: "Pro football received its greatest boost when Red Grange, the most publicized college player in history, stepped directly from the Illinois campus into the Chicago Bears lineup five days after his last college game.

"The Galloping Ghost drew pro football's first sellout crowds in Chicago and New York and created great excitement on coast-to-coast tour." The year was 1925 and the Giants were born as New York's first professional football team.

Sport parallels the history of the great world — we are reminded of the inhumanity of war, the blessings of peace, periods of prosperity and "You Can Help Smash That Line—the Bread Line" for men thrown out of work in the great depression of 1929. The Notre Dame All-Stars played the Giants at the Polo Grounds the following year, proceeds to the Mayor's Official Relief Committee on the Unemployed and Needy. The Irish came away with their lives and the committee with $115,153.

From one Hall of Fame great to another—Ernie Nevers, the Stanford star who challenged the Four Horsemen and Seven Mules and, with the Duluth Eskimos, played all but 29 minutes of 29 games in 1926, 28 of them on the road. The Eskimos wore greatcoats on the street, as a photograph attests, to publicize the games.

Sammy Baugh, his greatest years ahead of him, stands front and center in the 1937 All-Star squad photograph. His was a storied career in the books at Texas Christian University.

But a gleaming football of polished anthracite coal is a reminder of a controversial chapter back in 1925. The Pottsville

Maroons defeated the Chicago Cardinals 21-7 for the world championship. It was later noted that the Maroons had played a "world title" game against the Notre Dame All-Stars that year in Shibe Park, Philadelphia, thus violating the territorial rights of the Frankford Yellowjackets, ancestors of the Philadelphia Eagles.

Since the Cardinals played two fewer games than Pottstown, the Chicago team extended its schedule, a victory over Milwaukee being so farcical that the quarters were shortened *to* five minutes. Chicago then claimed the title, the anthracite football being Pottstown's rejoinder.

Was it worth it? "The club to whom the season's championship is awarded shall receive as a trophy 18 gold footballs with proper engraving on them, at a cost not to exceed $10 per ball," state the bylaws of that era, "and a pennant suitably lettered, at a cost not to exceed $37.50. The cost of the balls and pennant shall be borne by the league." This is not to denigrate the men who played the game. They were the greatest of their time.

Off the field the league edged past respectability into status. Up to 1933 the championship was awarded by a league meeting after the season and, as any student of history could predict, this led to controversy and some unpleasantness, as in the case of Chicago and Pottstown above.

And so, in 1933 the next great leap forward occurred when George Preston Marshall, a man usually described as flamboyant, successfully offered a resolution splitting the league into two divisions, Eastern and Western, a playoff between the leaders at season's end to determine the champions.

The first six Super Bowls failed to match the closeness of the initial championship game under that setup, the Chicago Bears defeating the Giants 23-21 on two touchdown passes by Bronko Nagurski. The following year the Bears and Lions met in the final game of the season with 10-0 and 10-1 records. The Bears won 19-16 and a week later duplicated the triumph for the title and the first undefeated, untied regular season record in NFL history.

Paralleling the exhibits along the wall, the rotunda's inner circle offers "the Red Grange of the Gay Nineties" Lawson Fiscus, "the Samson of Princeton," who in 1894 starred with

Greensburg, Pennsylvania, at $20 a game and expenses, which made him professional football's top wage earner.

Records of the Latrobe football team, 1895-1907, adjoin the documented debate, "The first pro? Fiscus or Brailer?" As if to prove that memory is seldom strictly chronological, the "Timmie" award of the Washington, D.C. Touchdown Club, first awarded to Baugh in 1943, stands over a light bamboo ball from Burma, "possibly representing the world's oldest game of football." (Players in a circle attempt to kick the ball without allowing it to touch the ground.)

Owners always strike a hard bargain. It is good to remember for the novice player. "I hereby agree," says a document in Spencerian script faded by the years, "to participate in all regularly scheduled football games of the Pittsburgh Athletic Club for the full season of 1893. As an active player, I agree to accept a salary of $50 per contest. I will play for no other club."

Americans are called, among other things, a nation of headline readers. It used to be that was all that was required. A 1906 newspaper account of "the first and perhaps fiercest of all football rivalries" reads:

"Tigers are Champions/ One of Hardest Fought Battles in Football History/ Tigers 13, Bulldogs 6/ Massillon Scored Five Points in First Half/ And in the Second Half Ripped Canton's Line/ To Pieces—Made Great Gains Around Ends and Toyed With Bulldogs Generally."

The trophy cases now abbreviate the great moments, from Wilbur "Fats" Henry, 1917 player-of-the-year at Washington and Jefferson; Walter Camp tackle in 1919, tackle on all-pro teams, 1921-23, through recorded comments via telephone from Thorpe and Minnesota Viking Jim Marshall recalling his 1966 wrong-way run with a recovered fumble against San Francisco.

Just as the deeds of some of the 74 men enshrined thus far in the Hall of Heroes are commemorated before you reach the Hall itself, so some careers span transitional periods of the game. Along the wall opposite the reminder of the Rams' last days in Cleveland hangs a huge banner, "Steamrollers, 1928 World Champions," recalling the era of coonskin coat and hip flask.

And beneath it is the number seven uniform of the remark-

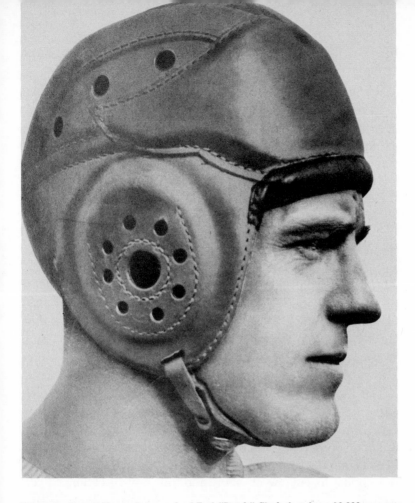

This is the *Detroit News* photograph of Earl "Dutch" Clark that drew 10,000 requests for copies before it appeared in *Life* magazine. The photo, like the man, remains the symbol of pre-war football.

able Earl "Dutch" Clark, a Hall of Fame quarterback who saw the Portsmouth Spartans become the Detroit Lions.

Ten thousand people used to jam the stands to see him at little Colorado College in Colorado Springs. It is not to be confused with Colorado University. After Clark graduated in 1930 the crowds shrank so drastically the school finally faced reality and ripped out 2,500 seats.

Clark scored an even 100 points his senior year and was named All-American by the Associated Press in spite of his obscure alma mater. He joined the Portsmouth team, quit for a year to

coach in Colorado, then rejoined the Spartans, following them
to Detroit: He was All-Pro his first five years, leading the league
in scoring with 55 and 73 points back when touchdowns came
harder. Some said he was as good as Grange. He drop-kicked so
many points he grew an ingrown toenail and switched to a kicking boot of hard rubber.

Clark also wore buckskin gloves in cold weather to protect
fingers broken in sandlot and college play. This was surprising
because Clark was his team's leading passer. "I know I can't
throw the ball as well with gloves," he said, "But I'd fumble more
and couldn't throw the ball at all without 'em."

But most astonishing of all, Clark was almost totally blind in
his left eye. None of these handicaps affected him. In 1934,
playing both ways, he led the Lions to seven consecutive shutouts to open the season. The following year they beat the Giants
35-0, and he threw only five passes in the playoff. Clark scored
a 40-yard touchdown in that one.

The Lions were basically an infantry-attack team, complete
with "KF-79," the touchdown-scoring play in Columbia's Rose
Bowl upset of Stanford. Dutch's pro coach "Potsy" Clark—no
relation—observed, "Dutch is like a rabbit in a brush heap when
he gets into the secondary; he has no plan, but only instinct and
the ability to cut, pivot, slant and run any direction equally
well."

Instinct or no, he was regarded as one of the brainier players.
Those who called him the greatest of all time said, "If Clark
stepped on the field with Grange, Thorpe and [George] Gipp,
he would be the general."

He was named All-League quarterback in six of seven years.
His percentage completion record of 53.5 must be compared
against a league average of 36.5 in 1936. He was so highly
thought of that he became the Lion's playing coach. When he
retired after a battle with management, he came back to coach
the Cleveland Rams to an overall 16-26-3 record. "Dutch," it
was explained, "didn't have a guy like himself to help him out."

A self-effacing man, Clark resisted all attempts to publicize
himself. There are those who said this cost him great fame. But
ability wins out, one way or another.

In 1936 a newspaper photographer wandered around the

Lions' practice field:

"I was moving around, taking shots, when I happened to get a side view of one player. I didn't know it was Clark. But I noted the strength of profile and attractive design of the helmet. The head looked Romanesque and gladiatorial."

Printed in a newspaper, Clark's photographic profile drew 10,000 requests for copies. The Lions inserted 9,000 prints in programs, later received 7,000 more requests. The photo, like the man, remains the symbol of pre-war football.

Unlike Clark, Ray Bray is not a Hall of Fame member. But the number 84 uniform he wore through ten seasons with the Chicago Bears is on display. He played in four championship games, two of more than passing historical interest—the 1940 rout of the Washington Redskins, 73-0—perhaps the most famous NFL championship game and ironically the most lopsided. Few remember that the Redskins gained revenge just two years later.

The 1942 Bears became the second team in NFL history to go through the regular season unbeaten and untied. Like their 1934 counterparts, who lost the famous "sneakers contest" against the Giants, they came up short in the title game. Baugh threw one touchdown pass, Sid Luckman none in a 14-6 triumph for Washington that had been heralded as a duel of great quarterbacks.

Even before the seasons stretched from August exhibitions to January Super Bowls, the championship games were decided in winter weather. Two factors shaped the outcome of the 1948 clash between the defending champion Chicago Cardinals and the Philadelphia Eagles. One was the snow; the other was Steve Van Buren. A photo shows him running over a player. He did that well enough to lead the NFL in four of his eight years in the league, setting a ground record that stood until Joe "the Jet" Perry and Jim Brown wiped it out. Surprisingly, he said he was one of those who couldn't play well when he was injured. Not so coincidentally, he was injured in four of his playing years.

Although he dropped people in their tracks, he was a college track man and remained the Eagles' fastest runner for 50 yards.

"Van Buren, who may be the best running back that ever lived," wrote Red Smith, "was a barefoot kid out of New Orleans, whose early life was devoted largely to shying rocks at street lamps. Thanks to his accurate throwing arm, New Orleans was,

The offense of the Philadelphia Eagles championship teams of the late 1940s was supposedly so simple it could be diagramed on a paper bag. Its key play—give the ball to Steve Van Buren.

for years, one of the darkest cities in America."

He was a blocking back at Louisiana State University until his senior year. Then Alvin Dark, who later became a major league baseball star, was drafted; and Van Buren ripped apart the Southeastern Football Conference, causing the Eagles to drop him.

With Tommy Thompson passing to Pete Pihos and Van Buren busting up the middle, the Eagles became champions in 1948 and 1949. "A superbly integrated gang of old pros," they were called.

Their coach, "Greasy" Neale was "so tough," said Van Buren, "I won't sit next to him on the bench." But Van Buren was pretty tough himself. When he ran over and flattened one of his blockers, an opponent picked up the Eagle and said, "Now you know what it feels like."

The year after scoring the playoff's only touchdown in the snow against Chicago, Van Buren waded through a sea of mud brought about by torrential rains in Los Angeles. The Eagles won 14-0, a record-setting two playoff shutouts in a row, and Van Buren's 196 yards bested the entire Los Angeles offense.

Rumor had it that he showed up as an Eagle rookie wearing no shoes. That was a canard. He wore shoes but no socks. Years later, invited to make the principal address at the Philadelphia Sportswriters Association banquet, he arrived resplendent in a new sport jacket.

"Called on to speak, he not only arose but hoisted one foot to the top of the speaker's table and proudly pulled up his pants leg," wrote Red Smith. " 'Look,' he said, 'I got socks.' That was his speech."

When he turned up late for practice one day, Neale slapped him with a fine. Van Buren protested he was in the whirlpool soaking out an injury. "Don't go bathing on my time," snapped Neale. "Take the whirlpool on your own time."

"I got the injury on your time," said Van Buren.

Neale backed down. After all, he called Van Buren "the greatest halfback I ever coached."

The Van Buren uniform included a one-piece fiber crown replacing the sewn leather helmets of the pre-1940s. A listing of championship game scores beginning in 1933, next to a chart portraying the evolution of the helmet, demonstrates how the game and the uniform changed together from the strictly functional equipment modeled by player-coach George Halas of the 1920 Decatur Staleys, with a jersey "ribbed to enhance ball-handling," to the $225-plus material worn by Kansas City tackle Buck Buchanan in 1970: kangaroo leather shoes, nylon cleats; metallic, polyurethane pants; waterproof molded plastic pads; aluminum "birdcage" mask. The end is not yet in sight, for artificial turf and developments unseen will dictate continuing changes.

But despite changes from the simple equipment of the low-scoring pre-championship days, through the advent of plastic helmets in the 1950s to the nylon-coylan jerseys of the Super Bowl, the indomitable spirit of the sport remains constant. The other constant reflecting that spirit is Halas. Treat of pro football and you cannot escape him.

Their recognition by the Hall, peripheral though it may be, accents the specialization of the game. Neither man does anything except kick. Much of Groza's kicking prowess was demonstrated while he was an All-Pro tackle. Baugh set punting records while starring as quarterback; he also played a whale of a defensive game. But that was decades ago. Today, said Detroit's controversial tackle, Alex Karras, the game is populated by specialists who whinny on the sidelines, "I keeck a touchdown."

All along, the Hall of Fame is instructive in more than football. A George Blanda exhibit demonstrates that the darkest hour before the dawn can stretch through the years. An All-American under Bear Bryant at Kentucky, Blanda was sweet-talked by Halas into signing with the Bears. Their East European ancestry was a bond; Luckman, Johnny Lujack and Bobby Layne, all Bear quarterbacks, were not part of the future, according to Halas. That was true, but Blanda was disheartened and mishandled. His brightest moments as a Bear came as a kicker, but he saw himself as more. At 31 he was retired after a lackluster career. After a year as a civilian, he was given a second chance with formation of the AFL, but his deeds at Houston were dismissed as triumphs among minnows. He was traded to Oakland as back-up to Daryle Lamonica.

Then at 44 and in his 22nd professional season, Blanda became a household word. On October 13, 1971 the Raiders were trailing hated rival Kansas City 20-10, when Blanda took over at quarterback with 8:51 in the game. He passed 60 yards to a touchdown to Fred Biletnikof. With 2:53 remaining, he kicked a field goal to tie the game. It was his 265th professional field goal, his 1,609th point, both breaking Groza records, and it was witnessed by a full house and a national nighttime television audience. It was the sort of thing boys dream of; particularly one boy named George Blanda.

But it was to be expected. The previous season, we are reminded, Blanda saved the day in five successive games, breaking
a 7-7 tie with three touchdowns and a field goal in a 31-14 win
over Pittsburgh. A week later he tied Kansas City 17-17, with a
field goal as the clock showed three seconds left. Cleveland fell
November 8 to his 14-yard touchdown pass and a 52-yard Blanda
field goal with 1:34 left. A week later his touchdown pass beat
Denver 24-19 with 2:28 in the game, almost a comfortable
margin of time. He capped it all on November 22, beating San
Diego quarterback John Hadl in the final AFL All-Star game,
January 17, 1970, as he led the West to a 26-3 victory.

A swatch of astroturf in the Hall leads to the present—symbols
of the 26 National Football League teams, the result of the
merger. And all of this — the humble beginnings with Hefflefinger, the millions represented by the merger — came about
through the deeds and dogged faith of the men enshrined in the
Hall. You are face to face with them, each represented by a bust
and an action drawing, the 74 for whom comparative records
mean nothing, only determination by the selection committee
that each represented the best of his era.

Appropriately, after the Agajanian, Stenerud and Blanda exhibits emphasizing the "foot" in football, the first bust seen in
the Hall of Heroes is that of Ken Strong who kicked his way into
immortality.

But Strong, who booted 147 points and 36 field goals with the
New York Giants, was more than a kicker. A 1928 All-American,
he set a collegiate record of 3,800 yards gained with New York
University and led the nation's scorers with 153 points. NYU
subsequently dropped football, perhaps a logical end for a team
called the Violets, but Coach Chick Meehan's squads in the
twenties were nationally ranked.

At 205 pounds, Strong was characterized as a great blocker,
passer and team player with spirit. Wally Stephens called him
"the best football player I ever saw." And Grantland Rice, the
veteran sportswriter who christened the Four Horsemen, said,
"With the possible exception of Thorpe, he can do more things
better than any back I ever saw."

There is a saying, "penny-wise and pound foolish," meaning
the tight-fisted deprive themselves of enjoyment, adventure and,

Grantland Rice, the legendary sportswriter said, "With the possible exception of Jim Thorpe, Ken Strong can do more things better than any back I ever saw." Strong's booming pre-game drop kicks frequently psyched out the opposition.

ultimately, money itself. When Strong was graduated from NYU, he was approached by the Giants. Attempting to save a few dollars, a Giant official offered him less than the club was willing to pay. Strong signed with the Staten Island Stapletons. "The depression was on," he said, "and the owners' attitude was 'I'm doing you a favor.' Today, the players do the owners a favor."

Strong also played baseball. He injured himself crashing into a fence in an exhibition game. A doctor allegedly removed the wrong bone in his wrist, finishing Strong as a passer.

The Stapleton team folded four seasons after Strong joined it, and he crossed over to the Giants, where he belonged. In 1933 he kicked a field goal against the Bears. The Giants were offside. He kicked again. The Giants were offside. The third time the kick counted and the Giants held on for a 3-0 victory. Bill Owen, brother of the Giant coach, failed to block his man on each attempt.

Next in line is the photo of "Automatic Jack" Manders, idol to a million schoolboys, kicking the field goal that kept the 1934 Bears undefeated. He played for Halas.

And then there is the uniform of the awesome Doug Atkins, six feet eight inches, 275 pounds, whose 17 seasons as a regular, full-time performer is a record. He started as a Cleveland Brown and wound up his career as a New Orleans Saint in 1969, but he played twelve years for Halas and the Bears.

A cast of Baugh's record-setting hand calls up his duels with Luckman, Halas and the Bears. The almost pathetically small and battered shoulder pads of Y. A. Tittle along with the green-and-white uniform he wore as a member of the original Baltimore Colts, represents a challenge the NFL beat back, not least because one of the weakest franchises, the Chicago Rockets, attempted to operate in Halas' Chicago.

The two strongest franchises, Cleveland and San Francisco, came into the NFL in 1950 when the AAFC folded. Baltimore disbanded, then came alive again with the transfer of a team from Dallas. An American Football League championship ball symbolizes the history of that league before it merged with an establishment personified by Halas, largely on terms favorable to the NFL. These included payments of $1,000,000 indemnities to each of the older league's team—a kind of apology for breathing.

Not that the AFL was without its superstars. Lance Alworth of San Diego and later with Dallas, is remembered here for breaking the supposedly unassailable record of Green Bay's Don Hutson by catching at least one pass in 96 consecutive games. He was shut out in game number 97, opening the 1970 season.

One reason for the AFL's reputation as a Mickey Mouse league is that it gave new life to NFL rejects. Gino Cappelletti was a University of Minnesota quarterback. He tried his luck for a season as a soccer player in Canada after graduation. He put in two years in the service, then he signed as a free agent with the AFL's Boston Patriots in 1960. As a wide receiver and place kicker he led the league in scoring for five years.

Jim Norton is recognized by the Hall not because he was with the Houston Oilers when they won the championship in the AFL's inaugural season, but because stepping down as the league's leading pass intercepter, he carved out an eight-season career as punter while Houston's fortunes faded. He was the only original Oiler still active when he retired in the spring of 1969.

A replica of the John T. Riddell Memorial Trophy, presented to the top AFL team by the Professional Football Writers of America, looks shiny enough as it stands in the Hall, but next to it is the number 15 jersey worn by Green Bay's Bart Starr, who had a role in diminishing the trophy's luster.

After Starr and the Packers socked it to Kansas City in the first Super Bowl in 1967, Green Bay Coach Vince Lombardi was asked to compare the Chiefs to the NFL's top teams. This was during the post-game interview in the bedlam of the locker-room. Lombardi, a gentleman, parried the question, then ignored it. The question was repeated. Exalted and tired, he finally acknowledged the query, "All right, the Chiefs don't measure up to some of the top teams in the National Football League. Is that what you wanted me to say?"

This was quickly translated as a put-down of the AFL. Some sources now describe Lombardi as gloating. Others imply that the observation was gratuitous. Some misquote for emphasis. It is fair to remember that Lombardi was only being responsive when he answered a persistent question, that he did not look for or seem to welcome the opportunity—and that what he said was probably perfectly true.

Near the Starr jersey are the shoes of kicker Ben Agajanian, who was 45 when he made his last point for the San Diego Chargers. Before that he journeyed from the Los Angeles Dons in the All-American Conference to Philadelphia, Pittsburgh, New York, Los Angeles and Green Bay in the NFL to the Los Angeles Chargers—for such they were before moving south—Oakland and San Diego in the AFL. Headliners vanished while he kept rolling along, the soul of persistence.

Records, it is said, are made to be broken. Near Agajanian's shoes is the soccer-style footwear of Kansas City's Jan Stenerud. In 1969 another "unassailable" record fell when Stenerud kicked sixteen consecutive field goals, breaking the mark held by Cleveland's Lou Groza in 1953. The Norwegian-born Stenerud, who drifted into football by accident while attending Montana State University on a skiing scholarship, became football's premier place-kicker. But he knew the bottom of despair when he missed two field goal attempts in the longest professional football game ever played, a double-overtime playoff won by the Miami Dolphins in 1971. The winning kicker was another foreign-born, a tie salesman from Cyprus named Giro Yermenian.

When the coach asked him why, he said, "Every time Strong kicked, my man lifted his eyes to heaven and said, 'Please, God. Don't let him make it.' I couldn't hit a guy who was praying, could I?"

In the sneakers game against the Bears the following season, Strong scored two touchdowns on glittering runs, kicked a field goal and three conversions. He could drop-kick as far as he could punt. A favorite ploy for psyching the opposition was to set Strong to drop-kicking before the game—from the 30, the 35, 40, 45—finally from beyond the 50. It set the other side to thinking about their chances, not favorably.

In 1938 he fractured three transverse processes in his back. But the following season he kicked two field goals and Ward Cuff kicked one, as the Giants shut out the College All-Stars 9-0.

Strong underwent an operation for ulcers in 1940. But the Giants called him back as a kicking specialist when he was 37. His son told him he had never seen him do anything except kick. So as the team romped over Washington, Strong asked quarterback Tuffy Leeman, "How about letting the old man run with the ball?"

He hit the wrong hole, bounced off and picked up a gain. Returning to the huddle, he said, "I just ended my career as a running back." But it developed that his son hadn't made the trip and wasn't there to see the run.

Following his retirement, he was brought back to coach the Giant kickers. "I put in 17 years of pro football," he once recalled. "I would have earned $100,000 more than I did if I came along ten years later. At that, I was hot stuff. When I broke in with Staten Island, I got $500 a game and an apartment for the season. There were a lot of Stapes, good ones, who were lucky to get $50 or $60 a game."

It was Strong's view, however, that if the players are paid more, the sport itself did not necessarily benefit. Strong believed progress "turned a grand old game into a circus, complete with limited duty semi-players, specialists who perform like trained seals at a crack of a ringmaster's whip."

No ringmaster's whip was required for Tom Fears, whose bust is next in line in the Hall. A nine-year star with the Los Angeles Rams, he caught 400 career passes for 5,397 yards. The only rookie ever to lead the NFL with 51 receptions, he then caught 77 to break Don Hutson's record, and then broke his own with 84. He caught a record 18 passes in one game. He was All-Pro from 1948 to 1950, leading the league in receptions each year.

Fears played on the 1950 Rams team that set a single season scoring record of 466 points. Three times during that period the Rams led the league in scoring. They scored 48 points in the third quarter against Detroit that year and rolled up 64 touchdowns over the season, gaining 5,420 yards—both records.

He scored all the Rams' touchdowns in the 24-17 playoff win over Chicago. The following year he caught a 73-yard touchdown pass that beat Cleveland in the playoff.

"We could score on anyone," said Fears. "We could score for a lot of reasons. We had the two best passers in football, Bob Waterfield and Norm Van Brocklin. We had Deacon Dan Towler, Tank Younger and Dick Hoerner as our bull elephant backfield, and we also had a quickie backfield in Glenn Davis and Vitamin Smith. Elroy Hirsch and I were the ends."

On October 30, 1949 the Rams introduced the modern pro attack against the Bears. Fears and Bob Shaw were outstanding receivers. From Green Bay the club acquired Hirsch, called "Crazylegs" as a college All-American at Wisconsin. He had suffered a severe head injury, and Clark Shaughnessy, the Ram coach, wanted to keep him away from the heavy traffic. So he placed him far out on the flank instead of at his normal halfback post. With Fears spread out on one side and Shaw in close, the "three end offense" was born. Today the positions are called split end, tight end and flanker.

The only reason Waterfield and Van Brocklin didn't rewrite the record book is because they shared quarterbacking duties. Beyond Fears' statistics is the fact that he was a clutch player, reserving his catches for third downs and the final minutes of the game.

"He was a game-breaker," said Van Brocklin, "a guy who always came up with his best play when you needed it most. He was a winner."

He didn't have much speed, but the six-foot, 220-pound Fears ran his patterns meticulously. "If the play worked," he recalled, "Van Brocklin would say in the huddle, 'O.K., Tom. What do you want next?' If it didn't work, he'd say, 'Shut up, Fears. What do you want, Hirsch?'"

Fears learned about pressure early and often. He was born near Guadalajara, Mexico, the son of a mining engineer. He remembers hiding under the bed during bandit raids before the family moved back to the U.S. when he was seven.

His college career at Santa Clara was interrupted by World War II. He served three years as a bomber pilot and finished his college career at UCLA.

Fears combined his pro career with parts as a bit actor in Hollywood movies, standing in for Clark Gable in all the distant action in 1951's *Across the Wide Missouri* and playing the Russian pilot who gives Humphrey Bogart the victory sign in the last reel of *Action in the North Atlantic*.

After packing it in with the Rams, Fears went to Green Bay as an assistant under Vince Lombardi, who was putting together the Packer dynasty of the 1960s.

"I spent five years with Lombardi," he said. "You can't help but learn a lot from him." Then he went to Atlanta with Norm Hecker, another Lombardi assistant. Hecker was first coach of the expansion Falcons.

When New Orleans joined the league the next year, Fears went after the head coaching job and got it. The team tied a record for an expansion club, winning three game its first year. He ran a tough camp, collecting $4,150 in fine money, which went toward building a $15,000 handball court for the team.

The biggest individual fine was $1,000 for "premeditated

carousing." A player made bed check, then skipped out. "Players never change," said Fears. "I think they look upon breaking training as a challenge."

The New Orleans Saints were made up of the usual expansion players — expendables from other teams and draft candidates. One of the good ones was Doug Atkins, acquired from the Bears. Atkins brought with him a dog named Rebel.

"He's a pit bull and a hell of a fighter," said Atkins. "Matched him with a Doberman, and the Doberman gave him fits for four or five minutes, but ol' Rebel never quit. Why, he can fight full speed for 35, 40 minutes, and he finally wore that Doberman right down. Got him down and probably would have killed him, but ol' Rebel ain't got any teeth. Had to gum that Doberman until he quit."

So it was with Fears' Saints, a writer pointed out. "They have unlimited courage and enthusiasm, but not enough teeth." After feuding with the general manager, Fears was dismissed midway in his fourth season.

"He did a fine job getting the team off the ground," said the owner, "but we needed a change." That year, Fears was inducted into the Hall of Fame.

3 PAPA BEAR AND
THE BISCUIT MAN

George Halas and Jimmy Conzelman—it's appropriate that these two old rivals should occupy niches near each other in the Hall of Heroes. Both played football in the early decades of the century, both contributed mightily to the legend of Chicago football as players and coaches, and both coached Chicago teams to NFL championships.

The similarity ends off the field. Halas, once called possessor of "a personality as daring as twin beds," is an original inhabitant of the Hall, the sole survivor of the group of men who met in Ralph Hays' auto showroom. "Papa Bear," as he is called, is founder of Halas University, where as many as 600 men who played for him gather at an annual party. "He didn't invent pro football," goes the saying. "It just seems that way." A patriarch, he remains active in the league more than half a century after he helped found it.

Conzelman was an original too, but of a different sort. The football helmet was only one of many hats he wore in a career as athlete, coach, songwriter, actor, showman, singer, advertising executive, composer of the epic "How to Take a Biscuit Apart and Put It Together Just Like It Was," and businessman.

Each was a sight to see on the sideline, but the activity exhilarated one and consumed the other.

Halas was a 25-year-old former end at the University of Illinois, where Walter Camp named him a second-string All-American, when he represented the Staleys as player-coach at the founding of the league. "I loved sports from the time I was old enough to cross a Chicago street by myself," he said.

Staley, the team's sponsor, forsaw the day when professional football would be too big for Decatur and told Halas to relocate to Chicago, offering him a $5,000 stake in return for the team playing one season under the Staley name. Fifty years later, that franchise officially would be worth twelve million dollars.

In between those years, Halas coached 327 winners—more than any other football coach amateur or pro, won 11 conference titles and seven world championships, and produced in 1934 and 1942 the only teams to finish a regular NFL season undefeated.

His greatest thrill and biggest disappointment involved championship games—the incredible 73-0 rout of the Washington Redskins in 1943 that made the T-formation famous, and the 30-13 sneakers game loss to the New York Giants in 1934.

Through it all, the man who introduced some of the game's greatest to the pro ranks—Red Grange in 1925, Sid Luckman in 1939, Gale Sayers and Dick Butkus in 1965—presented a familiar figure on the sidelines wearing a brown business suit, overcoat and a battered fedora he sometimes removed to kick in fury or in glee as he followed the ball and the officials up and down the field, hollering and protesting. When he quit for the final time, at the age of 73, he said it was only because arthritis in his hip "progressed to a point where I simply cannot move about quickly enough on the sidelines."

That arthritis dates back to an injury playing baseball. As a New York Yankee he powdered a hit off Rube Marquard in an exhibition game. He stretched it into a triple with a daring slide but collided with Marquard and hurt the hip. The Yankees let him go after he batted only .071 but found a suitable replacement for him in right field—Babe Ruth.

Conzelman followed a different route to the Hall. He, too, was a spectacle as he roamed the Chicago Cardinals' sidelines during the 1940s wearing baggy gray flannels, unpressed tweed coat and flopping galoshes, tossing his grey mane and chain-smoking cigarettes.

Some of his players said he communicated his nervousness to them. But he parlayed what was then called "the dream back-field"—quarterback Paul Christman, Charley Trippi, Elmer Angsman and Pat Harder—into the Cardinals' only world championship in 1947.

Halas' sideline exhibitions reflected his love for the sport, but Conzelman said, "I die every game, and a thousand times during the game. I don't know how much longer I can take it." And he retired.

He was the finest schoolboy athlete in St. Louis history before World War I, excelling at football, baseball and basketball. He promised to be the greatest quarterback ever at Washington University in St. Louis before the first World War interrupted his career.

Conzelman received national attention as quarterback for the 1918 Great Lakes Naval Training Station team that won the mythical national championship, defeating the Mare Island Marines in the Rose Bowl. One of his receivers was George Halas. Another Naval Station recruit that year was Jack Benny. "His idea of comedy then was to play the violin with one pants leg rolled up to the knee. Funny," said Conzelman, "it always got a laugh."

He returned to college for his final year, turned pro with Halas at the Staleys and went on to other professional teams in Providence, Rock Island and Milwaukee.

"Some of the teams had only two or three days of practice," he said. "That was a pretty rugged game we played in those days. The Staleys practiced six days a week. I made $1,800 my first season.

"The sport was considered such a lowly occupation that I returned home without telling anyone what I'd been doing. Only my family knew about my playing football."

He paid the NFL $50 for a Detroit franchise and gave it back for nothing after he and his partners lost $30,000. Two years later it was sold for a quarter of a million dollars. "That alone," said Conzelman, "should show you how I handle my business affairs."

Football couldn't absorb his abundant energies. He played baseball and managed a pro team in Rock Island, published five songs ("They are collector's items," he once said. "I believe I am the only collector who has any."); set himself up as a sculptor's business agent in New York's Greenwich Village and boxed with a top professional named "Philadelphia" Jack O'Brien, who unsuccessfully tried to get him to turn pro.

As great a natural athlete as he was, Conzelman understood that you must learn a sport from the ground up. The first time he put on the gloves with a professional, "I weighed about 160 and he weighed 118. He hit me about 40 times and I never laid a glove on him. Finally I was so winded I couldn't go on. I held up my hands and said, 'Hold everything. Let's start at the beginning. Give me lesson number one. Show me how to stand.'"

He applied the same lesson to music. Starting from the beginning, he learned to play the ukulele and progressed to the piano. "I'd try the succession of chords on the uke," he said, "then find them on the piano and finally add enough of the melody to create the impression that I knew what I was doing." He organized a dance band and put together two more to handle all the business.

In the early 1930s he published a weekly newspaper in a St. Louis suburb and wrote advertising copy and newspaper and magazine articles. Conzelman denied football was a character-builder. "There's just as much of a character building agent in parchesi if it brings together boys under proper supervision. It isn't the type of game but the associations that games bring about that count."

He got into coaching when his alma mater asked him to take over. It was suggested by some that he hadn't been a serious undergraduate, cutting classes and the like, and so wouldn't be the right kind of coach.

"I never heard of such a thing," said a loyal aide. "The idea of insinuating that Jim Conzelman isn't qualified to build character. Who is better able to build character, who knows the importance of building character better than a man who hasn't got any?"

Whatever the argument, Conzelman coached the team to a Missouri Valley championship in 1939, although he joked, "There

Jimmy Conzelman functioned as quarterback, coach, raconteur, songwriter, advertising man and promoter. But most memorably, he gave the Cardinals their only modern-day championships.

was a time when we considered the season a success if the team showed up. We always had what we regarded as a dangerous territory. It was any place inside the stadium."

The owner of the Chicago Cardinals was a man named Charles Bidwill. He was a great fan of the Bears. Once when the Cardinals were on the road he stayed home to watch the Bears play. But even he tired of seeing his team trampled by the Bears.

Conzelman joined the club in 1940. His three-year record was eight, 22 and three. He quit in 1942 to become an assistant with the St. Louis Browns baseball team, which proceeded to win its only American League pennant. Meanwhile, when training camp started up for the Cardinals, only 11 players appeared and only three of them knew how to put on their own equipment. In a game with the New York Giants they were one player short of the required squad number, so they put a uniform on a team trainer. They lost ten games that year and went through another winless season when they merged for the season with the Pittsburgh Steelers during the war year of 1944.

Conzelman returned in 1946 and the team won six, lost five. The next year Charley Trippi, the Georgia All-American, joined the club for the then unheard of salary of $100,000 and the "dream backfield" was born. The team won nine and lost three, taking the national championship. The next year they were 11 and one, but Conzelman retired to become an advertising executive because the "game took too much out of me." His teams won 30 out of their last 35 games, counting exhibitions, and 13 out of 14 league games.

He knew the value of effort and hustle. "One year the Bears finished first and we finished fourth. Yet our statistics showed that we had averaged one more yard a play than the Bears had. We couldn't understand it. How could we gain more yards per play than the first-place team and still finish fourth?

"Well, when the complete league statistics were released, we found out why. The Bears had run 120 more plays than we had. By getting in and out of the huddle quickly, by getting the play into motion faster, they had, in effect, done what a good salesman does. They had shown more hustle, they had 120 more calls than we did. It paid off for them."

Conzelman, who died in 1970, also knew the importance of being prepared. Although he was connected with football most of the time from 1914 to his retirement from the sport, he developed his other talents in case football didn't offer him work. And he understood the need for keeping sport in perspective. In 1942 he made a speech during commencement exercises at Dayton University "on a young man's mental and physical approach to war."

"Cultivate an acquaintance with violence," he said. "Challenge it, meet it, laugh at it." The following year the university gave him an honorary degree and the speech was distributed in an estimated 3,000,000 copies. But that was a wartime effort.

Conzelman also wrote an article for *Collier's* magazine called "Who's Yellow?" criticizing fathers who forced their sons into sport when they were inclined otherwise.

Although the 1947 team was a world champion, the professional game even then was not at all as organized as it is today. The crucial final game of the season was against Halas and his Bears. The Cards knew that the Bears' left halfback could be sucked in by the right end, leaving his territory unguarded.

So they put in a special play, making Babe Dimancheff their fastest man, a right halfback for the first time. But Dimancheff didn't show up for practice. When Conzelman asked why, Dimancheff said he was at the hospital with his wife who was expecting their first baby.

"I asked him if it might be possible for him to drop into practice and just run through the all-important play that we had built around him. Babe said, 'Oh, Coach, I couldn't leave my wife for a minute at a time like this.'

"So I said, 'Babe, are you staying at the hospital around the clock?' He said he was, and he promised that he would come to practice when the baby was born. I said, 'Have you got a room out there at the hospital?' He said he didn't exactly have a room. I asked him if he had a bed in the waiting room. The Babe said, 'No, Coach, I'm sleeping in a chair.'

"I couldn't help saying that this game Sunday was pretty important to all of us, and although I understood his feelings perfectly, it was pretty awkward to have the key man in our key play getting into condition by sleeping in a chair every night. He agreed it was a shame.

"Thursday came. No Babe. But he called up with a cheerful bulletin from the doctor and added he himself was resting well in his chair. But late Friday afternoon, there was a call from Dimancheff. He said, 'Great news, Coach. It's a girl, and we're naming her Victoria for the big victory we're going to win Sunday.' I congratulated him and asked him if he could come to the meeting that evening so we could diagram the play for him on the blackboard. He said he'd be sure to be there and would have a big cigar for me. . . .

"I was getting a little dubious about our chances, but Babe— after five nights sleeping in that chair—was bubbling over with

confidence. Came the game, we won the toss and elected to receive. The Bears kicked over the goal line. The ball was brought
out to the 20, and Paul Christman called for the key play. The
defensive left halfback of the Bears was pulled toward the center
of the field on a fake by our right end. Babe swung to the outside, followed by the slower linebacker of the Bears. Babe gradually pulled away from him and then at the 40 he turned, and
Christman threw the long pass. It worked perfectly. Babe
grabbed it and streaked for a touchdown, still bubbling. We
were off to the 7-0 lead we figured we needed and won 30-21.
The next week we beat Philadelphia for the championship. I felt
we owed it all to little Victoria."

Halas, who retired as a player in 1929, learned anew the value
of preparedness in the championship game against the Giants in
1934. Pro football was still a young sport in those days, although
there were big crowds on occasion.

They confirmed Halas' early impressions of what the game
could be when he saw people turn out to watch Thorpe run. He
had convinced any doubters when he signed Harold "Red"
Grange to a pro contract in 1925. Grange was the greatest of
All-Americans then, the most popular college athlete in the
country during a zany, jazz- and sports-crazy decade. Stadiums
were jammed to see him play. In his most famous game, against
archrival Michigan in 1924, the "Galloping Ghost" as he was
called, turned in the greatest performance of running with a
football the game has ever known.

In the space of 12 minutes he ran for four touchdowns in the
opening quarter of a game dedicating the school's new stadium
—95 yards with the kickoff, then on runs of 67, 56 and 44 yards.
The four times he scored were the only times he carried the ball,
after which he was taken out of the game. Returning in the third
quarter, he ran for a fifth touchdown and in the final period he
passed for a sixth.

The pass proved a point. Before the game, a Michigan critic
said of Grange, "All he can do is run." Illinois Coach Bob Zuppke
cracked, "All Galli-Curci," a famous opera star, "can do is sing."

His uniform number 77 carried a mystique from coast to
coast. Halas, whose Bears claimed the world championship in
1921 and finished second the following three years, counted on

Grange to build up the gate. For all the team's success, it was just about breaking even financially. Grange signed with the Bears after his final game against Ohio State and was put to work immediately, playing eight games in 12 days and earning himself $100,000.

Thirty-six thousand fans nearly broke down the gates to see him against the Cardinals in Wrigley Field on Thanksgiving; 8,000 turned out in a St. Louis blizzard; 35,000 attended in Philadelphia.

The next stop was the Polo Grounds in New York where the winning Giants were $45,000 in the red. Tim Mara, who had bought the team that year for $500, saying, "any New York franchise has to be worth that much," was willing to sell out but "where would you find anyone crazy enough to buy it?"

Grange was the turning point. Rain fell steadily through the week, but fans bought tickets faster than they could be printed —15,000 the first day, 25,000 the next two. Twenty-five hundred special police were called on to handle the mob; 70,000 fans jammed the stands, flowing out into the end zones as speculators got three and four times the face value of the ticket.

Grange played only a little more than half the game, carrying the ball 11 times, completing two of three passes and intercepting another for a touchdown. The Bears won 19-7. He received $30,000 for the game—$1,000 a minute—and while professional football's golden era was four decades in the future, its big-league potential was now beyond a doubt. Teams might lose money and franchises fail but no one who saw the hysterics at the Polo Grounds that Sunday ever again lost faith.

In 1930 Halas acquired Bronko Nagurski of the University of Minnesota, who made All-American both as a tackle and a full-back. At the time, the passer had to stand at least five yards behind the line of scrimmage. Three years later Halas and George Preston Marshall of the Washington Redskins pushed through a rule allowing passing from anywhere behind the line of scrimmage.

Halas immediately devised a play in which the mighty Nagurski feinted a run up the middle, drawing in the defense, then suddenly straightened up and passed. It worked well because Nagurski was described as a "man who runs his own interference."

And the Bears won the 1933 championship game 23-21 with the play against New York when the Bronk passed to Bill Hewitt who lateraled to Bill Karr for a 36-yard score. That set up a rematch a year later, the contest that lives in legend as the sneakers game. Twice during the regular season the Bears had beaten the Giants, and they were favorites to repeat for the championship.

The temperature that December 9 neared zero. The field was frozen as solid as a sheet of ice. Before the game a Giant player recalled his college team wearing sneakers on a frozen field and with better traction winning easily. "But where do you get sneakers on a Sunday?"

The bigger Bears dominated the first half 10-3 as both teams slid around the field, although two touchdowns by Nagurski were called back. But a little tailor and Giant fan named Abe Cohen went scurrying off to the Manhattan College gym and returned at half time with nine pairs of sneakers. The Giants scored 27 points in the final 15 minutes, winning 30-13 in spite of Halas' instruction to his player to "step on their toes."

"I think the sneakers gave them the edge," said Nagurski. "They were able to cut back when they were running with the ball, and we weren't able to cut with them."

"God bless Abe Cohen," said a Giant.

Twice more the Bears lost championship playoffs to archrivals Washington in 1937 and Green Bay in 1939. But these were only preparations for one of the great teams in football history, so indelibly stamped as "the Monsters of the Midway" that the memory persists as a cliche.

The T-formation dates back to the turn of the century as an obvious way to put the ball in play. But defenses caught up with it, and teams turned to the single- and double-wing formations, the short punt or Knute Rockne's Notre Dame box designed to spread out the defense, while the T only had power straight forward. Only Halas stuck with the T through the years, and in 1940 he decided it needed improvements. He brought in two college coaches described as geniuses—Clark Shaughnessy and Ralph Jones. As is often the case, the college imagination set fire to the pros. The two men devised plays which set a man in motion, forcing a defender to cover him and included a so-called counterplay, which struck against the direction taken by the man in motion.

To operate this was a young quarterback from Columbia University named Sid Luckman. He studied for hours with Shaughnessy, learning the fakes of the new T. His fullback was "Bullet" Bill Osmanski. George McAfee of Duke, quick as a water bug, was a halfback. The line was manned by giants like George Wilson, center Bulldog Turner, "Jumbo" Joe Stydahar and Danny Fortmann, the definitive watchcharm guard.

The team won eight games and lost three during the regular season. In the championship game they faced a Redskin team that had defeated them three weeks earlier 7-3. Studying films of the game, the coaches decided that the team that had held them scoreless was weak against counterplays and added nine of them.

A capacity crowd packed Washington's Griffith Stadium that day to watch their heroes, led by a young immortal named Sammy Baugh. The Bears won the toss and took the kickoff. On the second play of the game halfback Ray Nolting faked into the line. Osmanski faked to the left, took the ball and ran to the right. He found the hole blocked, so he bellied out to skirt end. A linebacker going with the fake was blocked easily. Osmanski had a clear path to the 35 where two Redskins waited. Charging across the field, Wilson threw a block so hard that he knocked one defender into the other, both of them flying to the sidelines. Osmanski scored and the biggest big-game rout in football history ensued.

When it was over, the score was 73-0. The Redskins were helpless. An end dropped a touchdown pass early in the game and Baugh was asked if that made a difference. "Yes," he said. "The score would have been 73-7."

Out on the West Coast, Stanford lost every game of the previous season. Now coached by Shaughnessy, it won the Rose Bowl using the T, and the stampede was on. At every level—high school, college and pro—coaches rushed to learn the new formation. Through the years, frills have been added—the wing T, the slot, the I, the double-wing T, but the basic formation dates back to its use that bloody Sunday in Washington and demonstrates the one immutable law of the game: whenever you hear of a new

Red Grange was the most popular college athlete of the sports-mad 1920s. He turned pro immediately after his final game at Illinois, embarking on a 12-day tour with the Chicago Bears that netted him $100,000 and demonstrated that professional football could command an audience.

formation or style, a "football of the future," you can be sure it was tried out somewhere before.

That revolutionary day would assure Halas of a place in the Hall of Fame. So would his longevity. But his contributions are endless. He was the first professional coach to call daily practices; the first to put an assistant in the stands to check the play; the first to use game films.

Even players who don't like him—"he throws nickels around like manhole covers," said one—respect him. He regards the Bears as his family, frequently doling out pay in small packages.

One player asked for an advance to buy his youngster milk. "What's his address?" asked Halas. "I'll send him a quart." But he is tremendously loyal, finding off-season jobs for players and helping them locate homes.

Through the years fans grumbled that Halas was too old and the game had passed him by. He would retire only to return when Jones, Paddy Driscoll or whoever failed as coach. His son "Muggsy" is president of the Bears. In 1970 his 88-year-old brother was still active with the team. "I wanted him to retire at 70 and I asked him again at 80," said Halas, "but he said, 'Who can do a better job?' I agreed. But I am going to insist he give up the work of traveling secretary when he is 90."

And the T-team of Luckman's was one of football's great dynasties. It repeated as champions in 1941, lost the playoff the next year, won again in 1943, lost again in 1944, won in 1946—an astonishing record when lineups were juggled and decimated through the four years of World War II.

A decade passed before the Bears were in the playoffs again, losing 47-7 to New York and another seven years before the championship came to Chicago. But in 1963 the Bears defeated the Giants 14-10 in a high-scoring era. Halas' brilliant defensive coach, George Allen, who went on to the Los Angeles Rams and Washington Redskins, devised a defense that allowed only ten points a game.

Winning or losing, the Bears remained one of football's major attractions, stamped with the rugged, dust-on-the-shoulders image of their city and their owner.

Gordie Soltau, an All-League performer with the San Francisco '49ers recalls his first game against the Bears. Opposite him was a defensive end of average size and fearsome reputation, Ed Sprinkle. He chatted with Soltau as they lined up and Soltau figured to himself, "He can't be so bad." On the first play Sprinkle tripped him. The Bear was solicitous and full of apologies, wondering how their legs got tangled up.

On the next play Soltau turned to look for a pass. A heavily taped forearm scraped his face and bloodied his nose. "Welcome," snarled Sprinkle, "to the NFL."

The boisterous spirit of the team, city and owner is captured in a story told by one of the game's roughest linebackers.

The one man representative of professional football from its early days to the Super Bowl present is George Halas, shown here with his one-time guard and later assistant Bear coach, Phil Handler. Halas has given his life to football as player, coach and owner.

"We were playing the Bears in Wrigley field," he once said, "when I fell on my face out-of-bounds, my two hands outstretched. Suddenly, someone stomped on them. I looked up and there was George Halas, that old man, jumping up and down on me. I saw red, and without thinking stuck my helmet into his belly and raked him up to the chin.

"I was ashamed of myself as I saw the old man staggering back. But he smiled and held out his arms. 'Son,' he said. "I wish you played on my team.'"

4/ TWO WAYS AND SIXTY MINUTES

The hand of George Halas was involved in the first sale of a pro football player from one team to another, and the player involved was Hall of Famer Ed Healey, who grew up on a farm outside Springfield, Missouri, where his duties included tackling stray hogs.

"So I started to play football" in high school, he told Myron Cope. "And it came sort of natural for me. Fear was most remote from my makeup. I mean, I loved body contact. I just thrived on it. I ate it up. If you have the stuff inside you, then you should be ignited by reason of being plugged by somebody."

After graduating from Dartmouth, he found himself loading beef in Omaha during 1920, when he learned there was a professional football team in Rock Island. He played with the Independents, as they were called, for two years. He nearly dismembered Halas in a game against the Bears, and the player-coach bought his contract for $100.

The game was rough-and-ready, particularly in Chicago. Healey recalled a day when he was going downfield to tackle Chicago Cardinal star Paddy Driscoll after a punt. "And then, holy cow! Out from the Cardinal bench, poured a group of men with rods on. They were going out there to protect their idol." It was, of course, the heyday of prohibition gangsters in the

"Windy City." Healey let another man make the tackle.

After Red Grange turned pro, a promoter named C. C. ("Cash and Carry") Pyle set up a rival league to the NFL with Grange as the star attraction. He offered Healey $10,000 to leave the Bears and come to New York. Healey told Halas, and the Bear ownership came up with enough money to keep him in Chicago.

It was, Healey figured, just as well. Both Pyle, who had been married three times, and New York seemed like fast company for him. He recalled a fellow tackle from Wisconsin who took Pyle's offer and "the last I heard, the poor guy was shot."

In any event, the Pyle league soon folded and Healey played out his illustrious career with Chicago.

Knowing when to stay put may be almost as difficult as transferring athletic ability into coaching ability. Just as a great coach may have been an inferior player, so the greatest player may fail as a coach—and never was there a better example than the man occupying the next niche in the Hall of Fame, Bob Waterfield.

"He is the best I've ever seen," said Sammy Baugh, the great passer who was also a top punter and defensive player in his early career with the Redskins. "Waterfield could do more things than anyone else—pass, run, punt, place-kick, kick off, receive, block and play defense." Don Hutson said he was the hardest safety man to handle. Perhaps the greatest all-around player ever developed in California, Waterfield led the then Cleveland Rams to an NFL title in his first year and became the only rookie ever to be unanimously named outstanding player in the league.

In addition to all this, he married his childhood sweetheart, movie star Jane Russell. It was said "he was probably the only man who could be married to her during the 1940s without becoming 'Mrs. Jane Russell.'"

In a career that ran from 1945 to 1952 he took the Rams from Cleveland to Los Angeles, playing for four different coaches, to four division and two world championships. But with all his talents, he failed as head coach of the Rams, resigning in the middle of a third losing season while the team he led to heights as a player had a one and seven record. It had lost 30 of 42 games.

Waterfield was born in Elmira, New York but grew up in Van Nuys, California. He was not a spectacular high school football player, going to UCLA more for his kicking than his passing prowess. Even in high school his classmates called him the "Great Stone Face." A sportswriter later said, "the last time he smiled was when he had a gas pain as a baby."

The stoicism had nothing to do with his popularity. He was an only child whose father died when he was young. Waterfield's mother allowed the home to be headquarters for fun and games, Southern California division.

He blossomed as a college junior in 1942, completing fifteen passes for 308 yards against Idaho. He scored 12 touchdowns that season, playing 617 of a possible 660 minutes on both offense and defense. His coach, Jeff Cravath, called him "the most complete player in college football." But the Bruins lost the Rose Bowl to Georgia 9-0.

His college career was interrupted by a brief stint in the service. It came to an end after he suffered a leg injury in a pick-up basketball game. He returned to college and a weak team, but led all college kickers with a 42-yard average for 60 punts.

Bob Waterfield attracted national attention in the East-West Shrine game in 1944 when he single-handedly sparked his squad to a 13-7 victory over the East. After setting up the team's first touchdown, running and passing, he scored the second, running 13 yards with a pass. His punting average for the game was 58.8 yards.

It is not recorded whether football's wise men were saying "it takes three to five years to make a professional quarterback" in those days. They say it now. It is one of those sayings that doesn't check out.

Waterfield immediately established himself on a par with Baugh and Luckman, then football's reigning quarterbacks. In the title-clinching game against Detroit he started things off with a 57-yard pass to Jim Benton. The duo set a league record of ten completions that day in a 28-21 victory.

Showing no respect for his elders, he frequently ran the bootleg play his first pro season, faking a handoff, hiding the ball behind his back and running with it. He worked it so successfully for a seven-yard touchdown against the Giants that officials were searching through a pile-up for the ball while he stood in the end zone. He scored four touchdowns as a rookie with the play. He also place-kicked 29 of 31 conversions. And he led the league in

A UCLA All-American, Bob Waterfield led the Cleveland Rams to a championship before accompanying them to Los Angeles—a move which made pro football a truly national sport.

interceptions with six.

The rookie had led the Cleveland Rams to their first and only pro title, but then came playoff day against Baugh and Washington. It was so cold that the musical instruments of the famous Redskin marching band froze and they were unable to play. Six boxcar loads of straw covered the playing surface before the game, but the field was still frozen.

Waterfield's passing proved the edge in a 15-14 victory marked by a strange play. Baugh attempted a pass from his end zone. The ball hit a goal post and was ruled a safety—the winning margin. The rule was changed the next year to make such a play an incomplete pass.

The weather wasn't uppermost in owner Dan Reeves' mind when he petitioned the other clubs for permission to move to Los Angeles. In those days of pre-jet travel, the idea of a team on the West Coast seemed implausible. But the other owners relented when Reeves pointed out that title or no title, the club lost $50,000.

The change of scenery didn't bring instant prosperity. The Rams competed for ticket money against the Los Angeles Dons of the newly formed All-American Conference and two immensely popular college teams—Southern California and UCLA. Reeves' losses the first year topped $160,000 and reached $207,000 in 1947.

Reeves was a rich man, but he couldn't lose that kind of money indefinitely. He took in partners for nominal payments and agreements to shoulder the deficit.

The team foundered on the field too, dropping to a six, four and one record its first year and doing no better than six and six the second season on the Coast.

Even a mediocre season offered excitement. The Rams lost 41-21 to the Bears in a free-swinging game that saw five players ejected. One of them was Ed Sprinkle, who was taken out for slugging Waterfield. After the game 228-pound Jack Matheson, a Bear end, came to the Rams' dressing room and shook down a little water boy for the game ball. Bob Snyder, the Rams' coach, threw a roundhouse right that knocked Matheson out the door and into the Bears' quarters.

Asked if the Bears finally got the game ball, Snyder said, "I don't thing they did."

You couldn't fault Snyder for his spirit, but his record was something else again. Reeves fired him and brought in Clark Shaughnessy as coach. The team improved somewhat, with a 6-5-1 record. But it continued to lose money—$253,000—and the rival Dons were averaging 10,000 more customers a game.

It all changed in 1949 when a squadron of talented players joined the club—Tank Younger from Grambling, Vera Thomas ("Vitamin") Smith and, in a trade from Green Bay, Elroy Hirsch. Finally the club learned that Norm Van Brocklin, a brilliant

University of Oregon quarterback, was officially eligible since he would graduate a year ahead of his class. He saved four games in relief of Waterfield as the Rams became the most exciting team in football, reeling off six straight victories.

They lost the championship in a downpour to Philadelphia, their speed and deception mired in a mud that didn't hinder the Eagles' Steve Van Buren.

Although he took the team to a division title, Shaugnessy was fired. The explanation was that he exhausted both players and assistants with a perfectionist's demand of 18-hour days. His replacement, Joe Stydahar, got along notably well with players and hired Hampton Pool to take care of the technical end of the game.

The rival Dons folded in 1950 as the Rams added Deacon Dan Towler to the backfield. The Waterfield-Van Brocklin offense broke all records, but the club televised its home games—this was before Bell's ban of the practice—and the team just about broke even at the gate.

Again Los Angeles lost the championship game—this one 30-28. The winners, ironically, were the Cleveland Browns, newly arrived from the departed All-American Conference.

Stydahar went to the dressing room determined to cheer up his players. They sat in silence, some weeping. He took one look around and walked out, tears streaming down his face. The game is played for more than money.

Blacking out home games the next year, the club ended its financial problems. It moved to another division title and beat Cleveland for the championship on a 73-yard Van Brocklin to Fears pass.

By this time, however, the club had developed cliques—one group of players preferring Van Brocklin, the other Waterfield. What's more, a rift developed between Stydahar and Pool. The coach was fired, and the assistant, a perfectionist in the Shaughnessy mould, was named to replace him.

The team won its third straight division title, losing to Chicago in the playoffs. It was Waterfield's final season and fittingly provided him with his most unforgettable game.

The Rams went into the third minute of the last quarter losing 28-6 to Green Bay. Two Waterfield field goals were their only points. The Packers were looking for desperation passes, and Waterfield dropped back. But Younger took the ball on the creaky, old statue-of-liberty play and ran 38 yards. Towler scored a little later, making it 28-13.

When the Rams faced a fourth down on the Packer 25 not long after, the experts were astounded to see Waterfield kick a field goal. What good did it do to make the score 28-16 with eight minutes left? Waterfield's reasoning was impeccable, "We need two touchdowns and a field goal. It doesn't make any difference what order they come in."

The panicky Packers fumbled. Younger fumbled right back. But a Ram end picked up the ball and dashed for a touchdown; 28-23, with five minutes left. The Packers punted to the Ram eight with two and a half minutes to play.

Two running plays picked up a first down. Waterfield hit Bob Carey for 20 yards. He hit Vitamin Smith for 30 yards. He hit Tom Fears for 26 yards. Smith plunged for four. Towler scored from two yards out. Waterfield converted for a 30-28 win. And there was still a minute left to play.

He retired with an avalanche of records. The passing accomplishments are to be expected, after all, he was a championship quarterback. But he also set an NFL record of 60 career field goals; most field goals in a game—five; most career conversions—311; most points-after touchdown in one season—54; most points-after touchdown in a single game—nine.

What the record book can't show, of course, was his great defensive play as exemplified by the Hutson praise. And one other thing:

". . . the stubborn belief in this corner is that Waterfield [was] the best, the trickiest and most valuable operator in the game," wrote Arthur Daley in *The New York Times.* "An unparalleled opportunity for appraising and evaluating the abilities of various T-formation quarterbacks was given this observer during a three- or four-year stretch when he described play-by-play of the pro games for television.

"He was never fooled by the fakery of Messrs. Sid Luckman, Sammy Baugh, Paul Christman, Tommy Thomason and all the other top-flight performers of that era. But Waterfield gave him conniption fits. . . . It was virtually impossible to follow the ball when he handled it."

Since he played for four different coaches with the Rams, Waterfield should have known the team was a coach's graveyard. He didn't need the money, having various business successes, including a movie production company with his wife. But he took the assignment with the catastrophic results already mentioned.

Once, after the team lost its sixth straight game he stood quietly in the dressing room. A reporter asked, "Have the owners talked to you since it ended?"

Waterfield, almost without expression, glanced down at his wristwatch, the black watch of the 1951 world champions he personally led.

"Not yet," he said, "but it's still early."

And when he was fired in the middle of his third season, Hirsch, then the general manager, had the grace to say, "I don't think it's fair to point the finger at one man and say it's all his fault." His successor was the team's eighth coach in 16 years.

Modesty was a tribute Waterfield shared with the Hall of Famer named all-time professional center, Mel Hein of the New York Giants. Linemen used to toil in obscurity. If that has changed, it was due in no small part to Hein, who developed a tremendous following in a career that spanned the 1930s, carried on through the early forties and saw him named All-League eight times.

It is frequently claimed that New York-based athletes get more than their share of publicity. This is true. New York, after all, is the communications capital of the world—home to national magazines and the television and radio networks. Hard as it is to believe today, the defensive team in football was paid little attention until the 1950s when Giant fans developed a love affair with their defensive platoon, particularly a middle linebacker named Sam Huff. He was featured in a cover story in *Time* magazine, and Walter Cronkite narrated a television program called *The Violent World of Sam Huff*. Other linebackers were rated equally good or better elsewhere, but the acceptance of the defensive team by the fans can be traced back to that period.

Today a supervisor of NFL officials, Mel Hein was a perennial All-Pro center with the New York Giants in the 1930s.

Hein came to New York in odd circumstances. As a high school football player, he dreamed of rowing crew at the University of Washington where the sport is a major attraction. An older brother enticed him to Washington State, however, where he was an All-American in his senior year.

He received an offer to play for the Providence Steamrollers at $125 a game. He signed the contract and put it in the mail. Then he discovered the Giants were offering him $150. The local postmaster couldn't help, but suggested that Hein wire the Providence post office and ask for the return of his letter. In

those simpler days, the systems seemed to work better, and Hein
got his contract back.

He married his college sweetheart and they set out for the
city in a jalopy loaded with crates, hat boxes and a violin. The
trip took ten days. Along the way heat melted butter over everything, a rainstorm turned the cardboard boxes into a soggy mess
and the bride fell asleep with her feet out the window in
Philadelphia.

Tired and confused, the couple took a wrong turn and wound
up on a one-way street at Grant's tomb. Hein had to wonder
about New York—when he stayed there the previous year after
a college game, his wallet and watch were stolen.

In spite of his All-American status he learned he was a football innocent, too. He was not an immediate starter. Called on
to spell the regular center against Brooklyn, he made his debut
with a hard tackle. On the next play the Dodgers lost ten yards.

From his linebacker post Hein figured the foe would be punting on third and 13, which was the custom in those days. His
job was to follow the end and block him for the punt receiver.
The end took off, Hein with him.

A football hit him on the back of the head. The pass, of course,
was intended for the end, the Dodgers electing to pass on third
down from deep in their own territory. It is standard procedure
today. Indeed, it can be asked why pro teams don't quick kick
for variety today, but it taught Hein that the pros didn't always
play by the rules.

He learned them well enough to star for 15 years. The acco-
lades were enormous, but in this day of hundred-thousand dollar
contracts, stock options and lucrative endorsements, it is instructive to remember what stardom meant in the depression era.

"1938 was my big year," Hein recalled. "I got $150 for en-
dorsing Mayflower doughnuts. When I won the Most Valuable
Player award some pipe company sent me a set of pipes. Free!"

At the end of the 1940 season the perennial All-League center
was honored with a day. The gifts included an automobile, silver
service, radio and traveling bag. On the field the results weren't
as good—Ace Parker led the Dodgers to victory.

The Dodgers were tough for the Giants. The next year they
beat them early in the season. A sellout crowd, typical of any

Giant-Dodger rivalry, gathered for the season's finale.

The play was ferocious. The wounded began to pile up around the Giant bench. In the second period Pug Manders intercepted a pass and returned it to the Giant four. He scored two bone-cracking plays later.

In the third period he intercepted another pass for a 65-yard touchdown. The play was rough enough that Hein and two other Giants went to the hospital afterwards and a half dozen others were under doctors' care. But for all the intensity of the game, there was a curious hum in the crowd. An urgent call for Colonel William J. Donovan to get in touch with his office was relayed over the public address system. There were further calls for military personnel.

The Dodgers won the game. The extent of Giant injuries might have provoked comment on other days, but not this time. The date was December 7, 1941—World War II had begun.

Hein retired and unretired twice. Like so many Hall of Famers, he could never get far away from the game he loved. Today he is supervisor of officials for the NFL.

 **A HANDFUL OF STARS**

It is one of the mysteries of life that talent sometimes appears in bunches. There was a period of great composers in music, for example, and immortal artists co-exist. So it was in professional football when a period running from the late 1930s to the early fifties was dominated by three quarterbacks, all Hall of Famers:

Sid Luckman of the Chicago Bears introduced the modern T-formation as the club, generally regarded as the greatest of one-platoon teams, won five Western Conference titles and four NFL championships, three within four years.

Sammy Baugh of the Washington Redskins, playing with inferior personnel overall, lasted 16 years, winning five Eastern Conference titles and two championships.

And Otto Graham of the Cleveland Browns, in the most remarkable show of all, won ten championships in ten years—four All-American Conference titles, six Eastern Conference titles and three world championships.

It might be called, with honesty, the era of great quarterbacks.

If teams led by Graham had the greatest success in the won-lost columns, it was said of Baugh, "He owns all the records." Time has eaten away at the full page once devoted to him in the NFL record book, but it doesn't appear likely that anyone will

ever better his 1943 season completion record of 70.3 percent.
He also put together games in which he completed 85.7 and 83.3
percent of his passes. By comparison, Virgil Carter of the Cincinnati Bengals led NFL conference passers in percentage of
completions with 62.2 in 1971.

Baugh also was regarded as the best defensive back in the
league when he first came up in 1937 and once led NFL punters
with a 51-yard average, booting out of the single-wing formation. Most of all, he demonstrated that the pass could dominate
a game until then pretty well given over to running.

Baugh could throw long, but he preferred shorter passes to
take his team down field. His great rival, Luckman of the Bears,
also could throw them any distance, but he was celebrated for
his longer tosses.

If Baugh showed that teams could pass at any time, anywhere,
it was Luckman who proved to be the right man in the right
place when Halas and Shaughnessy developed the modern T-
formation. It was enormously difficult to learn for players versed
in the single wing.

In his first season with the pros, Luckman was used generally
as a blocking back, while he absorbed the fundamentals of the
T from Shaughnessy out of a playbook more than 300 pages
thick.

The Redskins meanwhile stuck with the single wing, largely
out of deference to Baugh, but finally faced the day of conver-
sion.

When Baugh protested his inability to learn it, a coach recalled that at one point Luckman himself had burst into tears
over the complexity of the problem.

While Luckman and Baugh were working the knots out of
the T, Graham was performing in high school and college. When
he stepped into the pros, however, he became the winningest
quarterback.

He played his entire pro career under a moody genius named
Paul Brown. This leads to one of football's great unanswerable
chicken-and-egg questions: Was Brown the coach who made
Graham great, or Graham the player who put Brown in the
Hall of Fame?

Paul Brown was the only football genius to have a team named for him. His Cleveland Browns dominated and, some say destroyed, the All-American Conference. "We met a team from the big leagues" was the mournful verdict of one battered survivor.

The year after Graham retired Brown realized his first losing year in professional football, although he shortly was back on top. If the Brown system produced champions, it also unfairly cast a shadow over Graham's performance. The coach insisted on calling the plays, leading to a charge that Graham was a mechanical player.

It is unfair because no one questions Graham's intelligence. He called his own game as a single-wing tailback of All-American rank at Northwestern.

"In this one game, they were all set for the off-tackle play to the strong [right] side," he once recalled. "I told the center to lead me half a step to the left, and told the left end to take a couple of steps and cut for the sideline. There wasn't a man within ten yards of him. It was an easy touchdown.

"Later in the game, we worked the same thing. Two touchdowns on one play in one game. When I came off the field after the second score, the coach said to me, 'You really shouldn't make up plays in the huddle like that. Something could go wrong.' But he really wasn't chewing me out."

Graham continued to call the plays during his early years in the pros as the Browns piled on four championships in as many years. It was their total command of the All-American Conference that helped destroy it, fans deciding there was little point in watching also-rans.

Meanwhile, Brown came to the conclusion that quarterbacks had become stereotyped in their thinking. He sent in occasional plays, as does any coach, then moved on to control of the game by shuttling guards as messengers.

"I always had permission to veto any play Paul sent in," Graham said. "Any time I overruled him, though, I knew I had to gain as much or more with my play as he expected to gain with his."

Like Luckman and Baugh, Graham was an outstanding high school athlete. He studied five musical instruments, since both his parents were music instructors in Waukegan, Illinois. But, claimed Graham, "I was a typical youngster. When my father wanted me to practice, I would rather go out and play baseball or football."

He won letters in both sports and basketball as well, while excelling in golf, tennis and junior Olympic competition. He went to Northwestern on a basketball scholarship, becoming the first athlete to win All-American ranking in both sports the same year.

It was while he served as a naval air cadet at Chapel Hill, North Carolina that he learned about the T-formation while working with a Chicago Bear player. Because of wartime regulations Graham twice played with College All-Star teams against the professional champions. Both times the All-Stars won, an

"Automatic" Otto Graham won a championship in each of the ten years he quarter-backed the Browns. But like many great players, he found it impossible to transfer his genius to the teams he coached.

occurrence so infrequent that there were continued calls to end the series. In 1943 he set a series record with a 95-yard run, as the Stars defeated the Washington Redskins 27-7.

Brown assembled the Cleveland team meanwhile, largely drawing on men in service. He said he would have the most amateur team in the professional ranks, but he was looking for hungry players. Led by Graham, the Browns moved to a league championship in their first season.

"I was lucky to be able to start in a new league," Graham said. "If I was green, almost everyone else was green, too. We learned together."

And by way of demonstrating his astonishing versatility, Graham starred as a forward on the Rochester Royal team that won the National Basketball Association championship that year. He gave up basketball to concentrate on a football career that saw him win 90 professional games, losing only 15 and tying three. He recalled affectionately a play against Buffalo early in his pro career:

"We were ahead 14-0. It was in the days when I was calling the plays. We'd just stopped them on our one-yard line and called time-out. Now, one thing I'd always wanted to call was a screen pass from my own end zone, and I did.

"My teammates didn't want the play. I told them, 'If I'm rushed hard, I'll just throw it away. All we'll get is penalized half the distance to the goal. Half a yard.'

"Just before the snap, I saw their linebacker, who was supposed to hold Mac Speedie on the line. He started cracking in the middle and I knew we had it made. Speedie caught the ball on the goal line and ran 100 yards down the sideline."

But, said the critics, that was typical of play in the All-American Conference, "a Mickey Mouse league." The Browns were denigrated by NFL fans. After the AFC folded, Commissioner Bert Bell scheduled the Browns against the NFL champion Philadelphia Eagles in the first game of the new 1950 season. This was widely regarded as a move to put the all-winning Cleveland team in its place.

"That was the one game," Graham said, "when Coach Brown didn't have to say a word to us in the dressing room." It didn't help that the Eagle coach Greasy Neale said before the game, 'The Browns are a basketball team; all they can do is throw.' "

Utilizing an offense that ripped apart the famous Eagle defense with fullback Marion Motley and halfbacks Dub Jones and Rex Baumgardner, Graham passed freely to Dante Lavelli and Speedie. Lou "the Toe" Groza kicked field goals.

When it was over, the Browns had humbled the champions before 71,237 Eagle fans, 35-10. Graham completed 21 of 38 passes for three touchdowns and ran for a fourth. Neale said afterwards, "They sure have a lot of guns, don't they?"

Pete Pihos, a Hall of Fame end on the Eagle championship

teams of 1948 and 1949, was confronted by his wife after the game.

"What in the world happened out there?" she asked.

"Honey," he said. "We met a team from the big league."

The belittled Browns went on to tie the Giants over the regular season, defeat them in the playoff and then meet the Los Angeles Rams for the championship. The playing surface was like ice. The Rams, who had left Cleveland only the previous year, came up with what they believed was a secret weapon—tennis shoes with special abrasive soles.

On the first play, Waterfield passed to Glen Davis for an 82-yard touchdown. The Rams, holders of all the offensive records written that year, dreamed of a sneaker conquest like the Giants' 1934 triumph over the Bears.

But the first time a Brown was upended the Rams discovered that Cleveland too, wore the special shoes. Few people ever got up earlier than Paul Brown. Cleveland came back to tie the score, but Los Angeles led 28-27 with two minutes remaining and the Browns deep in their own territory. Graham had fumbled away a scoring chance. "Don't worry," said Brown. "We'll beat them."

It was then that Graham, called "Automatic Otto," demonstrated to NFL fans his ability to stop the clock. He clicked on a succession of sideline passes to receivers who then stepped out of bounds until the Browns reached the Los Angeles 16. Groza kicked the winning field goal with 16 seconds left.

Cleveland lost its opening game to San Francisco the next year, then won 11 straight for their second straight division title. They lost the playoff in a rematch with Los Angeles, 24-17. And with Graham passing Cleveland continued to win conference titles every year until his retirement — a record never even approached.

There was one flaw in all this. Detroit, coached by Buddy Parker and quarterbacked by Bobby Layne, exhibited a strange mastery over the Browns. Eight times, including two playoff games, the Lions defeated Cleveland. The eighth victory came in the final game of the regular 1954 season, 14-10.

Two weeks later the teams met in a rematch of the previous year's championship game. Graham ran for three touchdowns and passed for three more in a 56-10 rout, the most one-sided playoff after the 1940 Bear shutout of Washington. The Browns, adding insult to injury, intercepted six passes. As usual, the post-game comments cast little light on the shocker:

"We planned it that way," said Brown. "On any given day, this is the best football team I've ever seen." Said Parker, in a remarkable understatement, "Our luck ran out on us." Said Layne, "They kicked hell out of us."

But the big quote came from Graham, who announced his retirement:

"This is the way to go out, when you're on top," he said. "I am quitting because of the mental pressure. I have come to hate the pre-game tension worse and worse."

With three growing children and an off-the-field career in life insurance, business and television, Graham thought he was stretching himself too thin. But when Cleveland lurched through an unhappy exhibition season the next year, Brown coaxed Graham out of retirement with the expected results. Cleveland met Los Angeles for the championship before 87,000 people—a playoff record.

Graham passed for two touchdowns and ran for two more in a 38-14 victory shocking by its margin. He was "the greatest quarterback ever to play that spot," said Brown, whose own contribution was obvious. Cleveland had intercepted seven passes, an indication the coach had pretty well covered the Los Angeles pass routes.

Graham retired again, this time permanently. "So much depends on me," he said. "I don't worry about it during the week. It's the day of the game that gets me. Why? My nature I suppose."

In ten seasons he had passed for more than 24,000 yards and 184 touchdowns, exceeding the yardage piled up by Baugh over 16 years. But his outspoken nature opened him to criticism. Before making his comeback he wrote an article criticizing Brown for sending in all the plays, although he said it didn't affect their relationship when he returned to play.

He regarded Brown as a great coach, unparalleled in his ability to put together an organization. But he believed that the coach can as easily become stereotyped as the quarterback and that only the man on the field senses the flow of play. "Sometimes," he said, "Paul sent in a play two or three plays after it should have been called."

But when Graham coached his first College All-Star team against the professional champions he sent in the plays, presumably on the grounds that even All-American quarterbacks hadn't time to learn his system fully. Whatever his reasoning, it paid off with another All-Star upset, Detroit losing 35-19.

His comments on players came back to haunt him. He suggested that Brown trade Jim Brown, the all-time NFL rushing leader, because Brown didn't fake or block. "They'll never win anything," he said, "as long as Brown is their fullback. Now chew on that for a while." Graham did the chewing.

Cleveland proceeded to win the championship the following year. As All-Star coach Graham was critical variously of Bob Hayes—"great speed, but no moves or hands"— Gale Sayers and Johnny Sample—all of whom went on to win All-Pro recognition.

Perhaps it was only that Graham was so outspoken. Willing to comment almost any time, he learned the pitfalls of free speech. Sometimes the reaction was unfair. During the AFL-NFL rivalry he said that matches between the top teams of each conference would be toss-ups, although he believed that NFL strength predominated down through the roster. This was regarded as heresy.

Graham felt vindicated when the Jets upset the Colts in the third Super Bowl after Green Bay teams had trounced AFL entries the previous two years.

"I said the top teams in the AFL could give any team in the NFL a good game," he said. "If you recall, a couple of guys almost shot me. There is very little difference and has been very little difference between the top players in the two leagues.

"I coached many of them in the All-Star game and if they went into the NFL they were 'great' and if they went into the AFL, 'not so hot.'"

He really learned about the power of the establishment shortly after his retirement when he wrote an article saying some—but by no means all—pro players were dirty. He said his former coach and many teammates then quit speaking to him and that his comments cost him his off-season television show.

After turning down offers from major colleges Graham took over as head coach at the tiny Coast Guard Academy.

"All along I'd known that I'd like coaching," he said, "but for several reasons I had been reluctant to take any offer. I'd seen too many cases where coaching football turned out to be an intolerable pressure job—pressure from the alumni, the students and the administration. I didn't want any part of that. At most major colleges you've got to win or go elsewhere.

"Everybody wants to win, and nobody wants to win more than I do. I even want to beat my wife at croquet. But winning isn't everything. A coach, after all, has the chance to teach your son to be a good man, to live by the rules, to play clean and hard. And that is the most important thing."

But the pressure mounted in 1963. Graham's College All-Stars, led by Ron VanderKelen, a former Wisconsin star who memorized the game plan perfectly, whipped the virtually invincible Green Bay Packers of Vince Lombardi. Then his Coast Guard team made up of unrecruited boys went through their first undefeated season.

Three seasons later, Graham became head coach and general manager of the Washington Redskins who were foundering around in the lower reaches of the league. There were a few bright spots—he led the team to an even-split season, their first in years. He routed the New York Giants 72-14, breaking the NFL season record of 70 points.

"Ah, records don't mean anything. I only care about winning."

But some of his players criticized him. A major charge was that he didn't know how to organize practice sessions—the very point he emphasized as his old coach's great asset. His contract was bought up to make room for Lombardi and he returned to the Coast Guard as athletic director.

But for all the triumphs, the non-smoking, non-drinking Graham, of whom it was said, "His idea of a big night is eating chocolate ice cream," offered a final football philosophy:

"Football should be fun," he said, "for the players, the crowd and, yes, even the coach."

Graham, who frequently ran with the ball, once explained, "A quarterback should only run for his life. I have a wonderful wife and children, and I want to go on living."

Luckman, too, came along before conventional wisdom held that the more immobile the quarterback the better, and that good quarterbacks never left the pocket. Perhaps this view gained currency because there were so many clumsy quarterbacks around in the 1960s.

Surely, there was none like Luckman. A star at Erasmus Hall High School in Brooklyn during the 1930s, he received national attention. He chose Columbia University in New York City, an Ivy League school with no pretensions to football power, largely because of his admiration for Coach Lou Little.

That admiration was to deepen. Little was a gentleman of the sort cynics scorn, a believer that football was meant to be part of a college boy's education, that properly coached it instilled virtues like loyalty, courage and teamwork, the character to be modest in victory and gracious in defeat. Sometimes cynics get what they deserve. In 1934 Little took a derided, outweighed Columbia team to the Rose Bowl and upset 7-0 a Stanford team dubbed invincible.

Such moments were few and far between at Columbia. But Luckman proceeded to write further bright chapters in its football history. A fair runner and good passer as a sophomore, he spent hours working with the coaching staff. By his junior year in 1937 he was keeping games close with his passing and breaking them open on the ground. He passed for two touchdowns against Army, for example, and returned a kickoff 80 yards for a touchdown. Against Penn, he passsed for two touchdowns and scored another, picking up 144 yards on the ground and intercepted a pass.

By his senior year, *Time* magazine said, "Outstanding Eastern hero so far this season has been Columbia's Sidney Luckman, whose passing equals the best performances in football history. . . . Against Yale, halfback Luckman completed ten out of 17 passes (most of them on the run) for a total gain of 146 yards, scored a touchdown and kicked three extra points. He not only throws a 50-yard pass like a catcher pegging to second base, but feints his opponents out of position like a boxer."

Trailing Army 18-13 that year and bottled up for almost three

Sid Luckman, the modern T-formation's first quarterback, played a major role in revolutionizing the game, and won the affection of teammates and fans by demonstrating that a great player on the field can be a great gentleman off it.

periods by a team that recognized him as just about the only Lion weapon, Luckman completed three passes on a final touchdown drive and kicked the extra point. Final score, 20-18.

Football no longer requires the triple threat back—the player who can run and kick as well as punt. But Luckman exemplified the kind of man Little attempted to coach. "Everybody knows what a great player he is," wrote one newspaperman, "but few realize what a loveable, human kid he has remained. That simplicity is probably his greatest badge of all."

Unlike the situation at football factories, Luckman was admired by his peers on a campus where academic excellence rather than athletic ability is emphasized. "To these people, Luckman is no conventional hero," said a newspaper account. "He is a boy for whom they have an extraordinary feeling of affection . . . the whole of Columbia University shares it."

In those days college football players, particularly from Ivy League schools, did not necessarily go on to the pros. A few years earlier Jay Berwanger, the one-man team from the University of Chicago and first man ever to win the Heisman Trophy as the best college player in the country, turned down all offers from the pros. Luckman, too, had no intention of continuing a football career, planning to go into the trucking business with his brother.

But one rainy Sunday as he played ball, George Halas watched him from the end zone. And Luckman was no more able to resist Halas than many other young men through the decades.

As an indication of how the game, if not the level of talent has changed, try to imagine your favorite professional quarterback playing as a blocking back. And yet Luckman, the peerless passer of 1938, played that position in his first year as a pro, "blocking and making such a swell job of it," noted one reporter, "that runners like Joe Maniaci and Bill Osmanski have torn the opposition to shreds. . . ."

Luckman, a single-wing tailback, was also spending off-duty hours learning the intricacies of the T-formation—not only the plays but the techniques. "I had a terrible time with the pivots," he once recalled. "I used to practice for hours in my hotel room —spinning, pivoting and faking."

The results are already recorded—the 1940 season that shattered the concept of football as played up to then, with the man-in-motion T—"the Halas formation," Luckman suggested it be called—and culminating in the 73-0 Washington massacre in the playoffs. Europe was engulfed in World War II, and one account likened the Bears that day to "the German Army rolling through France. Dazed onlookers waited for the defenders to make a stand—in Belgium, at the Somme, at Dunkirk—but the Juggernaut kept rolling, rolling, rolling."

They were the greatest of the one-platoon football teams. In addition to Osmanski and Stydahar, Fortmann and Turner,

there were Ken Kavanaugh, the All-American end from Louisiana State University, Ray "Scooter" McClean and Duke's George
McAfee, a Luckman favorite. "He could punt, pass, run and
block," Luckman recalled. "Once he got by you, forget him. He
scored." And, too, there was a back from LSU named Young
Bussey, who would die as the U.S. battled for the Phillipines.

So much has been made of the 73-0 game, that other, almost
equally incredible performances are overlooked. In 1943 the
Bears came to the Polo Grounds and buried the Giants 56-7.
Luckman passed for 453 yards and seven touchdowns, a record
that stood for 11 years.

"Never since the Giants came into being in 1925 has any
team rolled up such a heavy score against them. And it was all
Luckman's doing," wrote Rud Rennie in the *New York Herald
Tribune*. "He came as close to being a one-man team as any one
can. . . . In all, the Bears, thanks to Luckman, set seven records."

To give you an idea of his accomplishments, Luckman missed
on only seven of 23 passes. He threw for 51 yards to Jim Benton,
then 44 yards to Connie Berry. Scoring passes completed
marches of 67 yards to Hampton Pool, 79 yards to Harry Clark,
76 yards to Benton again, 31 yards to George Wilson and 80
yards to Pool again. All of this against a good defensive team.

"It just happened to be one of those days that comes to a
player once in a lifetime," Luckman said. He went to the Giant
clubhouse to apologize to Coach Steve Owen. "If I'm gonna be
beaten," said Owen, "that's the way I want it done. I don't want
anyone to feel sorry and kick on first down. Since it had to happen, I'm glad you were the one who did it."

Over the years, the defense-oriented Giants had more successes containing the short passing game of Baugh than the
bombs of Luckman. The following year the playoff game was
billed as deciding whether Luckman or Baugh was the better
passer.

"The game turned into a rout," commented *Time* magazine.
The Bears won 41-21, but the question was still unanswered.

"Behind magnificent line play," the *Time* article continued,
"Luckman threw five touchdown passes. Fourteen times his soft
spirals connected, for 216 yards. But while all of this was going
on Baugh was off the field. Early in the game an accidental but

vicious crack on the head while tackling Luckman sent Sammy to the dressing room. He came back for the second half, barely time enough to toss two touchdown passes himself."

All of this happened, it must be remembered, in what was called an era of low-scoring games. And the team averaged 227 pounds in the line. Many of the players were in the service. Luckman himself played when he could find relief from duty in the U.S. Maritime Service.

How good were they? Once, playing Cleveland, the team kidded Luckman that his protection was so strong anyone could direct it. So, Luckman allowed each of them to call a play. They moved to the one.

In the huddle, Bulldog Turner told Luckman he had never carried the ball for a touchdown from an offensive formation. Turner came into the backfield and Bill Osmanski took his place at center. The play was over guard and Turner busted through for a touchdown.

"It was the only one he made from scrimmage in his life," Luckman said. "What a ball club we had."

The Bears met the Giants in the 1946 playoff. Two Giants were under suspicion for failing to report an attempted bribe. One was suspended. The other, Frank Filchock, in a magnificent display of courage played almost the entire game with a broken nose, choking on his own blood. A Giant fullback missed the game with a broken jaw. Halfback Frank Reagan was rushed to the hospital at half time with a fractured nose. Halfback George Franck also went to the hospital with a twisted shoulder. But the game was not decided until the final quarter when Luckman, who had not carried the ball all season, plunged up the middle, brushing off two tacklers, and scored. A field goal iced a 24-14 championship.

The team ran out its string. Luckman schooled Notre Dame All-American Johnny Lujack as his successor. But ten years later, the Bears felt that the retired Luckman, successful as a Chicago businessman, contributed so much as a part-time coach that they voted him a full share of their winning playoff money. He returned it with thanks to the pool for the Chicago players. The only way the story got out was through Commissioner Bert Bell.

Unlike many oldtimers, Luckman does not insist on the

superiority of yesterday.

"There's no comparison," he said. "Today's players are far superior to those of my day. They are bigger, stronger, faster, better coached all the way from the high school level, and they start football younger."

He also pointed out that the atmosphere was different. "Certainly we were dedicated to the game, but it wasn't the be-all and end-all factor in our lives. We weren't making a career out of it; we were using it strictly as a quick means to a secure end."

He recalled a game against the Dodgers involving Joe Maniaci.

"He was from Brooklyn, and Halas always started a boy when he played in his hometown. So Maniaci was the starting fullback.

"But it came game time and Halas couldn't find Maniaci. Finally, someone spotted Joe in the stand. He was in uniform, but he was also wearing one of those advertising sandwich billboards which read—'Come to Maniaci's Restaurant for Dinner After the Game.' "

In the endless debate over the greatest quarterback—Baugh, Graham or Luckman, newspapermen who had known Luckman from his schooldays on, confessed they could not look at him objectively. They recalled his modesty and his quiet charity. He invested $25,000 in a restaurant he knew would fail. "The guy who owns it was nice to me when I first came to Chicago," Luckman explained. "This is a great fellow. He had to be to be nice to a kid like me. Nobody even knew me then."

It didn't occur to Luckman that as a college star slated to play for the Bears he was certainly known. When the wife of a fellow player was taken ill, Luckman quietly paid the hospital bills and money for a housekeeper to look after the children.

"The funny thing about it," said the man who told the story, "is that Sid didn't think he was doing a favor. The guy was his friend. Sid figured it was his duty."

Offered money after he returned to Columbia to help coach, Luckman returned it. There are things money can't buy, he noted, but "my feelings toward Coach Little and the college are such that I can repay neither."

"Everything I have," he once said, "I owe to Lou [Little] and George [Halas]."

"Whatever Little and Halas gave to him," wrote Jimmy Cannon, "Sid Luckman canceled the debts. He is a guy who always pays his own tab and squares a lot of other people's checks. I want him on my side, I don't care what the proposition is. I don't know a finer man in sports . . . a graceful and gentle man, and his kind have always been scarce in this world."

The impact of one man on a sport is illustrated in another manner by a rawboned Texan named Samuel Adrian Baugh. George Preston Marshall was a laundryman—"Long live linen!" was his motto—who believed in professional football. But his Boston Braves lost money—even after he changed their name to "Redskins;" even after they won a conference championship in 1936.

So he moved to a neutral site for a playoff game, lost to the Green Bay Packers 21-6 in spite of Redskin runners like Cliff Battles, Ernie Pinckert and Riley Smith. What was needed was an accurate passer to get the ball to ends Charlie Malone and Wayne Millner.

Along came Baugh. He was an immediate hit. He established football in Washington so that through dreary years and lost decades, it remained one of the most successful franchises in professional football. The capital that would not support the baseball Senators turned out for the football Redskins.

It was largely due to Baugh. Is that an exaggeration? Listen to the words of Joe Carr, a league founder and president in 1938, after Baugh's rookie year:

"Through Washington's history-making first season in the league, there stood in bold relief against the entire personnel of the ten-team circuit one of the most astonishing performers the pro grid game has known, 'Slingin' Sammy Baugh. To this strike-tossing forward passer, the greatest yet to appear, went the plaudits of the nation. In one short season, his first as a professional, he became football's greatest thrill."

The curious part of this is that Baugh planned a career as a baseball player. He grew up in the west Texas town of Sweet-water. He spent more time as a boy practicing punting than he did passing, although he whiled away hours throwing a football through an automobile tire swinging from a tree.

". . . In the summertime I used to go on the football field by myself," he told Myron Cope, "and kick for hours. I'd kick at

For 16 years Sammy Baugh hurled the pigskin for the Washington Redskins, much of that time punting and playing defense. But his unassailable contribution was establishing pro football so firmly in the nation's capital that not even years of dreary teams dimmed fans' enthusiasm.

those sidelines and then run down and get the ball and kick it back. And especially after I got to TCU I got where I could kick the ball out of bounds inside the five- or the ten-yard line pretty good."

But he had played baseball all his life. A friend told him he could get a baseball scholarship to Washington State University. He ripped up his knee so badly sliding into second base that he couldn't straighten his knee and the scholarship to Washington State fell through.

He went to Texas Christian University with the proviso that

he play baseball, basketball and football. The years 1934-36 at TCU are understandably known as the "Sam Baugh era," although even he could not take his undermanned team to a Southwest Conference title. He kept getting better. In his sophomore year he passed for a .397 percentage. He upped that to .461. And as a senior he completed 109 of 219 passes for 1,371 yards and a .498 percentage, achieving All-American rank. He won three consecutive games with three touchdown passes each. Seasoned sportswriter Grantland Rice was so taken with Baugh he put TCU in his top ten years after Baugh graduated.

"The thing I'll always remember about Baugh," said a rival coach, "is that he didn't anticipate his receivers. He had such uncanny accuracy that he'd just send the ball like a bullet right where they were."

He also ran and punted, kicking for a 43-yard average as a senior, the year he played in the first Cotton Bowl game, throwing a 55-yard touchdown pass in a 16-6 victory over Marquette.

Pro football was unknown in the back reaches of Texas. Baugh planned to play baseball and take a football coaching job to fall back on if he didn't make it as a player. In Chicago for the All-Star game, however, "I talked with the rest of the boys and found that a bunch of them were going to play pro football" he recalled. "I found out that most of them were just like me—that they hadn't been out of the country too often themselves—and that I could play ball better than 90 percent of them. So I became more confident."

He signed with Marshall for $8,000. "Later I felt like a robber when I found out what Cliff Battles and some of the other players were getting," he said. But Baugh was worth every cent from the day he got off the plane in the Washington airport wearing the cowboy hat and boots Marshall urged him to buy for the occasion.

"Mah feet hurt," said Baugh at the first safe moment.

Many pro teams of the time sent out one man as the receiver, the others as decoys. That wasn't Baugh's way. He adjusted pass patterns to meet the defense and could find the open man. He threw the ball hard and once it hit a Redskin in the back of the helmet.

"Hey," said the receiver when he got back to the huddle, "I

wasn't supposed to get the ball on the play."

"Where I come from," Baugh answered, "if you're open, you better be looking for the football." He completed 11 of 16 passes his first game. Receivers dropped the other five.

Baugh immediately established credentials. Veteran Coach Greasy Neale said, "He throws strikes on the run. He never misses his target. The only way to stop his passes is to smear his receivers."

That didn't always work, though. Baugh took the Redskins into the playoffs against Chicago his first season in the NFL, still another shot at the theory that it takes years to develop professional quarterbacks. (He played tailback, of course, but it amounts to the same thing.)

The game attracted enormous interest and a sellout crowd as Baugh returned to Chicago where the previous summer he had led the College All-Stars to victory over the Green Bay Packers. "Washington has a capable, smart team," noted one newspaperman, "but Baugh is the magnet. Sammy made football popular in the national capital."

Three days before the game it snowed. Both teams wore sneakers on the skating rink surface. Players' fingers froze. The Bears banged up Baugh's leg early. With the score tied 21-all, Chicago was "watching Charlie Malone, our end, on the play that won the game for us," Baugh recalled.

"Malone cut down the field with Chicagoans all around him. I faded back on the run, and still on the run, heaved the ball— but not to Malone. Ed Justice was in the right flat, and there was absolutely no doubt about where he was headed." Washington 28, Bears 21. The game ended with a brawl that included players, fans and, in a shouting match, Preston and Marshall—a typical Bears-Redskins game of those days.

"Of all the years I played for Washington," Baugh said, "the early ones were the best. In the first nine years we played in the championship game five times."

Baugh still hadn't forgotten his first love, baseball. He signed as a third baseman with the St. Louis Cardinals, who assigned him to Columbus in the American Association. He was put on waivers at the end of the season. "I realized in my own mind that I couldn't hit," he said, "and I haven't put a glove on since."

The transfer to Washington and the presence of Baugh wiped out Washington's financial losses. There was a question, however, of how long the lean Baugh could last. He suffered a shoulder separation early in 1938, and the Redskins dropped to second place. "The quarterback could be hit any time up until the whistle blew," he recalled of those days. "And we got hit plenty. In fact, every quarterback was pretty well clobbered." A rule change was finally written in protecting the quarterback once the ball left his hands.

Meanwhile, Baugh was off on a five-year tear leading the league in punting. His passing records were eclipsed as the game changed, but his lifetime kicking average of 44.49 yards, season average of 51.3 yards and game average of 59 yards stood the test of time.

He was so popular that he took off time to make a movie serial, *King of the Texas Rangers*. "Easiest way I ever knew to make a livin'," he drawled. "And lots of fun besides. Reminds me of kids playin' cowboys and Indians. All you do is run around makin' faces."

Years later, when it turned up on television, he couldn't even remember if he got the girl in the end. "All I know," he said, "is they ought to burn the damn thing."

Perhaps the most famous anecdote concerning the early Baugh came when a coach, challenging his accuracy, said, "Hit that receiver in the eye." And Baugh answered, "Which eye?"

He became the inseparable friend of halfback Dick Todd, a Texas A & M product. Asked if Sammy would make an appointment, a friend said, "Baugh will be there, Todd willing." Married to a minister's daughter, Baugh named the first of their five children Todd.

Privately, he thinks Washington lost the famous 73-0 game to Chicago when it beat the Bears three weeks earlier. Some of the Bears were crying, he said. One told him, "You just remember—we'll be back." He also thinks Washington "left a lot of our games on the practice field" while the Bear workouts were stymied by bad weather.

He personally won the game when Washington beat Chicago in a playoff rematch two years later. "Baugh was a headache with the unexpected," said Halas. "It is a principle you should never kick against a strong wind if it can be avoided. But Baugh quick-kicked several times on third down with the wind almost dead in his face.

"We could not imagine he would kick, and he had us stalled. He tackled that wind like a sailor, not a cowboy." The Washington victory prevented Chicago from winning three straight championships.

Not until he had been in the league seven years did Baugh become a T-formation quarterback, further proof of his indestructability. The change did not come easily. "It's very difficult to get comfortable under the center after you're used to the single wing," he said. "Getting your feet right... doing certain steps." But after he made it, he said he could have bettered his 16-year record if he had always worked out of a formation which "a quarterback ought to be able to play in white tie and tails."

Cliff Battles, the great Redskin runner, quit football in a salary dispute early in Baugh's career. He never had more than one or two outstanding receivers. Many complained he put too much mustard on the ball. The team frequently was mired in mediocrity.

Baugh simply rolled along setting records. An opposing rookie asked, "How do you stop the guy? He throws such a quick pass, something like a pivot man in baseball making the double play. He gets rid of the ball so fast I don't think I could have gotten to him even if he didn't have any blocking."

In his twelfth year he disassembled a cocky young Giant team 41-10, completing 16 passes for two touchdowns and scoring on a quarterback sneak. That same year he set a league record completing 17 passes in a 59-21 slaughter of the Boston Yankees.

He seemed vulnerable because he never kept more than two backs back for blocking, preferring to send them out as potential receivers. His durability, a question when he first broke in, was at least partly due to his living habits. He seldom drank and never smoked, although cigarette endorsements added to the estimated $300,000 he picked up on the side. "Half goes to taxes," he drawled, "and half to Texas."

He maintained a 22,000-acre ranch to which he repaired

whenever he could. "I never missed the big cities," he said. The cowboy regalia worn for publicity purposes became standard gear. He learned to twirl a rope and soon was competing in rodeos. Once he helped teammates who violated curfew by hauling them up from the street after lights were out.

The 1947 Redskins set a league record when they allowed 367 points scored on them. They won only four games. But Baugh topped all passers that season, completing 210 passes for more than 2,900 yards.

A dream was realized when he was paired with the greatest receiver of the day, Green Bay's Don Hutson, in a charity game.

He threw one pass to Hutson.

"I caught the ball on the 40-yard line," Hutson recalled, "and crashed down on a turf that was as solid as concrete. They hauled me to the sidelines with a broken rib."

As Baugh broke his own records, passing for a .703 completion average in 1943, setting three all-time records two years later, he continued to be the greatest individual gate attraction in pro football. He defied retirement rumors, coming up with big games after he seemed finished. But after he found himself largely relegated to holding for points after, he announced he was quitting.

"I've enjoyed all my 16 years, but I think the time has come to quit," he said. "I know I can't play ball like I used to. When you feel you're not playing ball as well as you should, it's time to get out."

In his pro lifetime he completed more than half the passes he threw—1,709 of 3,016 for 187 touchdowns. "What I wouldn't give to be playing the role of a T-quarterback today," he lamented.

"I could last 20 years or more with nothing to do but throw. The single wing meant running with the ball half the time. You took a beating. And who hears of a T-formation quarterback blocking these days? We had to block and play both ways, too."

Recalling an era when he led the league in interceptions, he noted, "Playing defense and blocking is where you get hurt. Many a game I played the whole 60 minutes."

He spoke up for his rivals. "Cecil Isbell, Waterfield and Luckman would all be great passers playing today. The big difference is the receivers. Every club has 'em in abundance today. It goes back to scouting systems who dig up catching specialists. That's all they're paid to do. Pass receivers in my time had to play defense, too."

He took over as coach of Hardin-Simmons, a short distance from his home. Then he coached two tumultuous years for the New York Titans, a ragtail predecessor of the Jets in the American Football League. His teams there compiled a 14-14 record in two seasons. Dismissed, he went back to the ranch before returning for a stint as coach of the Houston Oilers. No matter what he did he spent as much time at his home as possible. He was not as glib as Graham, but he made his words count. He described a flanker candidate: "He has great speed, great moves, and hands like feet."

Appearing before a group of FBI agents during one of Washington's woebegone seasons, he said, "This is the best protection I've had all year."

Of a deeply religious linebacker he said, "Johnny knocks hell outta people, but in a Christian way."

He believed in tempering enthusiasm with realism. "When I was coaching Hardin-Simmons we played Auburn and Baylor and Ole Miss. Now we never went on the field with a defeatist attitude. We always thought we were going to win. But there were a lot of times I wouldn't have bet my ranch on it."

But the greatest passer searched for words when asked to explain what lifted him above the forgotten and anonymous players of earlier years.

"Maybe it's because," he started and then paused, perhaps seeing the six-year-old boy throwing for hours at the tire swinging from a tree. "Maybe it's because I didn't have a penny when I was a kid. I don't know. Maybe that was it. But I always wanted to be better, to be the best. I wanted to be the best passer."

COACHES ON THE FIELD

The best passer. Isn't that what quarterbacking is all about? To many observers, not until the appearance of Joe Namath did professional football offer a player who could throw the ball as quickly or as accurately as Sammy Baugh.

But ideally the position requires more than that. Leadership —the ability to hold a team together—is another attribute. So is football intelligence—the quality of knowing the right play to call at the right time.

It used to be that even more was expected of the signal caller. Hall of Fame quarterback John Leo "Paddy" Driscoll who died at age 73 in 1968, played safety, carried the ball, passed, kicked field goals and points after, and was the last of the great drop kickers.

Playing with the Cardinals and Bears from 1920 to 1929, he never weighed much more than 150 pounds. His records of four drop-kicked field goals in a game and 49 during his career still stand, as does his feat of twice drop-kicking the ball 50 yards. But he was no mere specialist.

After achieving All-American status at Northwestern University, he played on the Great Lakes team that defeated Mare Island in the 1919 Rose Bowl. All he did in that game was drop-kick a 30-yard field goal, get off a 60-yard punt, return nine punts for 115 yards and gain 91 yards carrying the ball. Walter Camp, who had watched them all up to that time, called him "the greatest quarterback I've ever seen."

In his first game at Northwestern Driscoll returned the opening kickoff 95 yards for a touchdown. He gave up his last year of eligibility to play baseball for the Chicago Cubs, batting .117 in a brief career as a second baseman.

He found himself in 1925 kicking to Red Grange right after the Galloping Ghost turned professional. Twenty-five times he punted in that game and 23 times the ball went out of bounds. Determined not to let Grange rip off a big runback, Driscoll saw to it that even the punts that could be fielded were hard to handle.

Boos poured from the stands. After the game Driscoll said, "I hated to hear them booing Grange. He's such a nice young man."

"They weren't booing him," said his wife. "They were booing you for not kicking to him so he could run."

Like many Hall of Famers, Driscoll could not give up the game he loved when his playing days ended. He coached high school ball before moving on to Marquette University. He joined the Bears' coaching staff in 1941 and even took over the head coaching job (if that was possible as long as George Halas breathed) from 1956-57, winning the Western Conference title his first year. He was one of the oldtimers on the Bears' payroll when he died, serving as head of research and development, as it was called.

That quality of leadership looked for in a quarterback was never better exemplified than with Bobby Layne, who entered the Hall of Fame after a 15-year career with Detroit and Pittsburgh. Although he came along decades after Driscoll, taking the Lions to championships in 1952, 1953 and 1956, he also could put his foot in the ball, winning respect as a Texas University All-American for his quick kicking prowess.

He also won a reputation as a party boy. Not all the headlines were made on the field. He came close to being the first citizen of Detroit. When he was found innocent on a charge of

Bobby Layne, the hard-living, dynamic leader of the rough-and-ready Detroit Lions, destroyed the aura of invincibility that surrounded the cold perfection of the Cleveland Browns.

drunken driving on the grounds that police misunderstood his Texas drawl for the slurred speech of the drunk, signs appeared over the "Motor City": "I'm not drunk, Judge. I'm from Texas."

But automobile giant Henry Ford II found Layne "one of the most complex and sensitive men I've ever met. I couldn't understand how he could play in such a rough game." Layne said of himself, "Nobody enjoys living like I do. I like to vibrate. I vibrate Sunday after a game, and I vibrate Monday night, Tuesday night and Wednesday. But after midnight Wednesday, nobody in the world but my wife can get in touch with me."

There may be something to the tall Texas talk of producing great football players. In 1948 Layne, who came from Dallas, threw his first NFL touchdown pass—a 48-yarder to Ed Sprinkle of the Bears. Sprinkle was from Abilene, Texas.

Buddy Dial was an 11-year-old schoolboy playing football in his backyard in Magnolia, Texas at the time. Fourteen years later, playing in the Cotton Bowl against the Cowboys, Layne threw to Dial for a Pittsburgh touchdown. It was his 188th in the NFL, breaking Baugh's old record.

Layne also broke Baugh's completion records with 1,710 for more than 25,000 yards. "He broke almost every record set by Baugh," said one commentator, "while closing in on every record held by W. C. Fields."

The Layne story assumed dramatic overtones early. When he starred at Highland Park, a Dallas suburb, one of his teammates was a quiet young man named Doak Walker. They went their separate ways after graduation but remained in touch through the mails.

Walker took a Southern Methodist team to a 7-6 lead over Texas in his sophomore year. With seconds remaining, Layne unleashed a touchdown bomb. The following years, with Walker in the service, Texas romped.

That set up a showdown with both men All-American candidates and the football-conscious in the state arguing through the night about which was the greater player—Walker who ran, passed, kicked and played defense, or Layne, the bullet passer. SMU won 14-13 as both men lived up to advance notices, but Layne was still chucking away at the end.

They were reunited with Detroit and perhaps Walker recalled their days as college rivals when he said, "Bobby Layne never lost a football game. Time just ran out on him." Layne set some sort of college record, winning 28 Southwest Conference baseball games without a loss, but there was never any doubt that football was his game.

Halas made a rare, monumental error about Layne. Sid Luckman was playing out his career with Chicago; Johnny Lujack was heir apparent. So Halas traded Bobby to the ill-fated New York Bulldogs. When that team collapsed, Layne went to Detroit. Lujack developed a sore arm and quit while Chicago searched but never found a quarterback like Layne.

One story demonstrates his unflaggable leadership qualities. He took the Lions to a championship, demonstrating his mastery over Otto Graham and Cleveland for the first time in 1952. The two teams met again the next year, Cleveland taking a 16-10 lead with time running out and Detroit deep in its own territory.

Said Layne in the huddle, "Jes block a little bit, and ol' Bobby will take ya right to the championship." Moments later he passed 34 yards to Jim Doran for the tying touchdown. Detroit went on to win.

The wild, come-from-behind game was a Layne hallmark. In 1957 he brought Detroit from a 27-7 third quarter deficit to a 31-27 victory. He beat Baltimore by the same score with two touchdowns in two minutes. Playing the Rams, both teams scored three times in the second quarter—42 points.

Small wonder then that when Layne showed signs of aging and so was traded to Pittsburgh, he cried. "It's the first time in my life I ever did that," he said. He rejoined Coach Parker, who earlier had left Detroit in a dispute with management.

He remained the peerless leader. Teammates responded to him as they had at Detroit. A favorite procedure was for Layne to take a rookie out for a night of carousing and then work him the following day until he was sick.

But the old magic was gone, to say nothing of the gifted personnel he played with at Detroit. Pittsburgh under Layne and Walker came as close as it ever did to a conference championship, but it fell short.

"Four years ago," said Layne, "I'd pop out of bed on Monday morning for a few rounds of golf. Now it takes me until Thursday to get out of bed." And so the man who said his ambition was "to run out of air and cash at the same time" retired to a career in oil and real estate.

Historians of the future probably will say that Layne's Hall of Fame peer Norm Van Brocklin made even greater contributions to the game after he retired as a player. Van Brocklin quarterbacked two teams to NFL championships—the 1951 Rams, on that celebrated 73-yard touchdown pass to Tom

When Norm Van Brocklin said, "A quarterback should only run from sheer terror," he convinced legions of naive coaches and fans that a quarterback improved his chances by being a stationary target. Only the successes of Roger Staubach and Bob Griese seem likely to undo the mischief.

Fears, and the 1960 Philadelphia Eagles, a team regarded as no better than second or third in the East but lifted to the title by Van Brocklin's awesome leadership.

The Dutchman—call him that or "Dutch" and anyone around pro football knows who you're talking about—is author of one of football's most famous sayings, "A quarterback should only run from sheer terror." Since he had won an NFL title and proved himself an inspired coach, this was widely assumed to be the essence of football wisdom. Quarterbacks of sound running ability through the 1960s were grounded by coaches and fans quoting Van Brocklin. Not until the successes of Roger Staubach and Bob Griese, opposing Super Bowl quarterbacks in 1972, did wiseacres really accept the obvious truth—if a quarterback can run well enough to pick up gains and avoid losses, it is better to encourage him to run.

To show you how silly and stereotyped football thinking can become, otherwise intelligent men said, "No scrambling quarterback ever won a championship." They overlooked two points: Quarterback is only one of eleven positions in football. Ten other good men are generally required on a title team. And secondly, quarterbacks usually identified as scramblers got that reputation because they had to run after inept teammates failed to block for them.

Van Brocklin himself learned to stay in the pocket under a particular circumstance. Born in South Dakota as one of nine children, he was taken to California as a boy. He starred in both football and baseball as a high school student and might have chosen baseball as a career if he hadn't lost years in the service.

He ran well enough to play tailback in high school. But when he arrived at the University of Oregon he was told by Coach Jim Aiken, "You run out of the pocket, and you're on your way home." Once, just once, he defied the coach. He took off for the sidelines during a scrimmage and was knocked into a hedge lining the practice field.

"Van Brocklin," screamed Aiken, "you got a million-dollar arm and a ten-cent head. Don't you *ever* do that again."

He remembered that all during his 12-year NFL career, nine with Los Angeles, three with Philadelphia, as he completed 1,553 passes for 23,611 yards and 173 touchdowns, with only 178 interceptions. He punted for a 42.9 average. And in all that time, he gained 40 yards running.

He came to Los Angeles on his own recommendation, writing a letter to Dan Reeves in which he said he had accumulated enough credits to graduate ahead of time. Reeves paid him $2,500 for the tip. The Dutchman always did things differently. He had asked a pretty girl for directions to the biology lab. She proved to be his instructor. He married her. "I got an M.A. in education," she later said, "and a Mrs. in biology."

He alternated with Waterfield at quarterback, as we have already seen, and the results, while productive, were not happy. He took over in 1953, winning a Western Conference title two years later, only to be slaughtered in Otto Graham's farewell appearance in spite of a 67-yard touchdown pass.

The following year Coach Sid Gillman made Billy Wade his starter, a mysterious decision explainable only because Wade didn't care if the coach called the plays. "I was set down," said Van Brocklin. "It was strictly a coaching decision."

He won the job back the following year, but he was unhappy. He was traded to Philadelphia, a team with so-so personnel. The team went two, nine and one his first year, seven and five—good enough for second place—his second and then won the conference and the playoff.

Leadership? Look at this. Five times during the championship season the Eagles trailed at half time, once by as much as 24 points. Five times Van Brocklin went to the blackboard in the dressing room, and five times Philadelphia came from behind to win.

He liked to throw the bomb. He once threw five touchdown passes of 30 yards or more in a single quarter. He threw two touchdowns against the Bears on passes totaling 145 yards.

He was called a coach on the field. Against the Bears, Tommy McDonald came back to the huddle with the information that the cornerback took his eyes off him on a pitchout. On the next play Van Brocklin faked the pitch and passed 40 yards to McDonald for a touchdown.

The key to the championship may have come against a New York Giant defense Van Brocklin called "harder than Japanese arithmetic."

The Eagles recovered a fumble on the New York 49. Van Brocklin remembered a trap play designed to fool Sam Huff, the Giants' middle linebacker. And he remembered that Huff was reading him when he called an audible—a change of signals at the scrimmage line. When he called "21," Huff, sensing a dive play, moved up.

Van Brocklin told the team he would sting Huff.

"One, 21," he called at scrimmage.

"Dive!" yelled Huff, moving up.

Van Brocklin stepped back with the ball, made an intentionally bad fake to Ted Dean and a better one to Billy Barnes.
Dean ran through the hole left by Huff, who charged in on the
empty-handed Barnes.

With the other defensive backs drawn in by Huff's call, Dean
roamed free in the backfield. Van Brocklin dumped the ball to
him for a touchdown and the Eagles went on to win, beating
Green Bay in the playoffs on two Van Brocklin touchdown
passes. He was named most valuable player in the league.

But when he was asked about picking a defense apart, Van
Brocklin said the expression was overworked. "The whole game
is primarily a matter of blocking," he said. "Get the blocking
and you're a great quarterback."

Critics said he was stubborn. Leading San Francisco by three
touchdowns, he passed on fourth down rather than kicking.
The 49ers took over and came from behind to win. Van Brocklin said only, "I'd do the same thing again."

He frequently challenged other players to a fight after the
game, but he never showed up. "I may have a hot head," he
said, "but it's not empty."

He retired in 1960, apparently believing the Eagles would
name him coach to succeed the retiring Buck Shaw. Told he
would be a playing coach, he made the retirement stick.

Then he was named first coach of the newly formed Minnesota Vikings. He said, "We have a dog or two from every club
in the league." But he cajoled the veterans, whose feelings may
may have been hurt when their old clubs released them, and the
rookies with a training camp in remote Bemidji, Minnesota,
"the only town I ever saw where the definition of a juvenile
delinquent is a kid who can't hit eight of ten from the free-
throw line."

Although he summed up the club's prospects saying, "it's
hard to say with a bunch of stiffs like that," he promised to win
games. And the Vikings, in the first game they ever played,
beat the history-rich Bears. The following year, Van Brocklin's
training camp was a combination of Marine boot training and

40 years with the Foreign Legion.

Quarterbacked by Fran Tarkenton, a man who played as though he invented the scramble, the Vikings kept improving. But in the middle of his fourth season, Van Brocklin quit as coach. "I've taken this team as far as I can," he said. He returned, after second thoughts, 24 hours later.

But he said, "I had great hopes for Frances. Just then he began to pull away from me." The following year Tarkenton demanded to be traded. Van Brocklin, fearing the team was hopelessly divided, resigned again. He put in a year as a football analyst for CBS television. Then he was named head coach of the Atlanta Falcons.

It seemed only a matter of time until he coached them to a championship. "To say Van Brocklin wants to win," wrote Larry Merchant, "is to say Picasso likes to paint pictures."

Wanting to win is as much a part of the quarterback's equipment as a fine throwing arm. But sometimes it is a long time coming. If you are born for greatness, however, you learn to wait.

Yelberton Abraham Tittle was a Marshall, Texas schoolboy who idolized Sammy Baugh. He was good enough to win a scholarship to Louisiana State University. In the summer of his senior year he was "kidnapped" by the University of Texas. They had a quarterback named Bobby Layne, and Tittle hightailed back to LSU.

He didn't set the woods afire there, making no better than second-string All-Conference. But he enjoyed some stickout days. He ran 60 yards for one touchdown and passed 62 for another in a 31-21 victory over Alabama. He threw 73 yards for a touchdown against Texas A & M and 80 yards for his team's only score against Georgia Tech in 1947.

He was drafted by Cleveland in the All-American Conference. It seems they had a quarterback named Graham, so they didn't weep when Tittle went to the newly organized AAFC Baltimore Colts, not to be confused with the NFL team you read about.

Tittle and the Colts learned together and quickly enough to tie for an Eastern Conference crown. They lost the playoff.

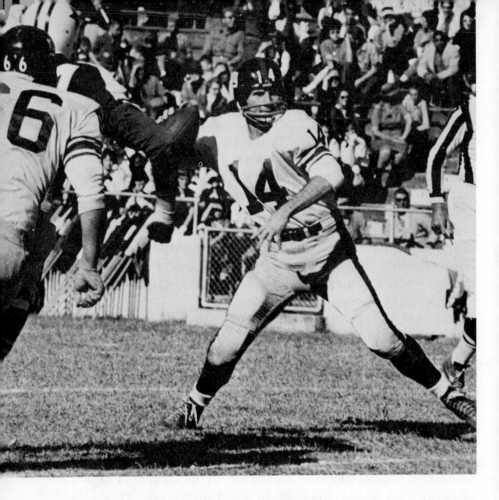

It was thought of by some that Y. A. Tittle, veteran of two pro teams, had left his playing days behind him when he joined the New York Giants in 1960. But Tittle's quarterbacking found him renewed glory on the most glamorous of pro football teams.

The following year they slumped. Coach Cecil Isbell was fired and Tittle benched. When the team folded (they were later reorganized from scratch) Tittle went to San Francisco.

Going to a new team is like being the new kid in school. Everybody else already has made friends. The reigning 49er quarterback was a happy-go-lucky left-hander named Frankie Albert. Sometimes happy-go-lucky. . . . When Tittle asked him for advice on a play, Albert said, "You seem to forget. You're after my job," and walked away.

But Tittle settled in, first alternating with Albert, with whom he later became friends, and then taking over. The atmosphere in the early years was relaxed. Coach Buck Shaw let the team set its own moods. Hit as he was attempting to pass one day, Tittle lofted the ball. It was grabbed over the heads of other players by a leaping, lanky player named R. C. Owen and the "alley oop" pass—an arching throw like a basketball shot—was born. But the 49ers couldn't win a title either in the AAFC or the NFL. Once they led Detroit 24-7 in the third quarter of a playoff and had first down on the Lions' nine. Four plays failed to score, and the Lions came back to win 31-27.

Shaw was fired and moved on to Philadelphia, Van Brocklin and glory. Albert took over as coach, succeeded by Red Strader, succeeded by Red Hickey. No championships. Hickey installed the shotgun formation, putting the quarterback at tailback where he could pass or run.

He decided the aging Tittle was expendable. Other teams in the league passed up the broken-down—concussions, a partly collapsed lung, smashed ribs, a broken cheekbone, broken wrists, a broken toe—baldish quarterback called "Mr. Clean" and "the Grey Eagle." New York acquired him for a tackle named Lou Cordielone, perhaps the single most lop-sided trade in football history.

First working in tandem with Charlie Conerly, who was even older, then taking over, Tittle led the Giants to three consecutive Eastern championships beginning in 1960. The playoffs were lost—twice to Green Bay, once to Chicago—but the team stood the world's richest, most competitive and most sophisticated city on its ear. Tickets to a Giant game became harder to get than for the biggest Broadway show.

"It's better than chopped liver," said Tittle. "I ask for a cigarette, the next day there's a carton in my locker. I shake hands, somebody slips me $50. I take a bow on the Ed Sullivan show—$500. I'm not giving that up until my arm falls off."

From literary salons to working men's saloons, the Giants were the talk of New York. Tittle, Frank Gifford, Sam Huff, Andy Robustelli, Jim Katcavage, Kyle Rote, Alex Webster—the team consisted of household names. Green Bay dominated the league but the Giants dominated New York, and Tittle dominated the Giants.

Playing a Washington team that had won six in a row, Tittle passed for seven touchdowns, tying a record in a 49-34 triumph. He completed 27 of 39, 12 in a row, for 505 yards, a high mark for the Giants.

The playoff losses to Green Bay were almost acceptable. Paul Hornung set a new standard scoring 19 points, and the Packers poured across 24 points in the second quarter in the first championship game played in the Wisconsin town. The next time around at Yankee Stadium, swirling, 30-mile-an-hour winds and a temperature that seemed even colder than the official 15 degrees hampered the Giants, a passing team. But the score was a respectable 16-7.

In 1963 it seemed the Giants' turn at last. The team averaged 32 points a game during the regular season. But the Chicago Bears, sparked by the emergence of Dick Butkus as the best middle linebacker in the league, had given up just ten points a game. Only the Bears lived up to their statistic on a frozen, ice-patched Wrigley Field. Once again, the Giants fell short, 14-10.

The following year the roof fell in. Trades sent Sam Huff to Washington and Dick Modzelewski to Cleveland. Coach Allie Sherman was determined to make the club his own, building around younger men. The Giants dropped their first game. In their second, against Pittsburgh, 270-pound John Baker belted Tittle in the end zone and left him kneeling, bloody and dazed, suddenly an old man beyond his 38 years. It was symbolic of the season—and seasons—to come. The previous year's conference champions wound up in the cellar, winners of just two games.

"I never wanted to be a mediocre player," said Tittle at season's end. "And last year I was mediocre." He retired to a successful real estate business and part-time coaching chores with San Francisco and New York.

Looking back over his career, he said he owed a great deal to Isbell, his first pro coach, who taught him the best place to throw is outside, rather than down the middle. Cecil Isbell knew a lot about throwing. He was blessed among NFL quarterbacks, for he threw to Don Hutson.

7 / THE END

It took more than two decades and squadrons of talents, but most of Don Hutson's records were gradually wiped off the National Football League record book. Nobody touched the mystique, however. Hutson deserves a Hall of Fame all his own.

He practically invented the qualities demanded of a pass-catching end. Brilliantly fast, he was a magnificent feinter. He could catch a ball on the fly or in traffic, with defenders draped on his slim, 185-pound frame. He could, and did, catch a touch-down pass after a run at full speed, step-by-step with a defender, wrapping an arm around a goal post so that he was whipped in a circle. He then reached up and grabbed the ball with his free hand. Falling, leaping forward, backward, he got the ball.

He looked as though he loped, until you tried to keep up with him. He had three speeds: fast, faster and fastest. The New York Giants routinely covered him with three men—one at the line of scrimmage, one deep, and a safety.

In 11 years as a pro he caught 489 passes for 8,010 yards and 100 touchdowns, leading the league as a receiver eight years. Thomas Edison once said genius was ten percent inspiration, 90 percent perspiration. Hutson, talented by birth, said "For every pass I caught in a game, I caught 1,000 in practice."

Time and other talents eroded most of the records set by Don Hutson, but decades after his retirement he remains the pass-catcher against whom all others are matched.

He always gave the credit to his passers—Dixie Howell in college, Arnie Herber and Cecil Isbell in the pros. "Whenever I turned around, I knew the ball would be there." But it is an understatement to say he helped them look good.

He is forever associated with Alabama and Green Bay, but he was an Arkansan. There was a pipeline to the Tuscaloosa campus in those depression days, and Hutson was one of eight Arkansans who found their way to Alabama's football team after he starred in basketball, baseball, football and track in high school. He once caught five touchdown passes in a single game for Pine Bluff.

A fellow Arkansan played "the other end" at Alabama. Hutson was so good that Paul "Bear" Bryant had to go into coaching not to be outdone. He became one of the greatest at Kentucky, Texas A & M and Alabama. The two ran a dry-cleaning business as undergraduates. They fared better than the customers.

"We didn't do great work," Hutson once said, "but we were tremendous salesmen." When the uniforms of the ROTC unit were soaked by rain the day before graduation, Hutson and Bryant received a contract to clean them. They worked through the night. After a trip through the steam presses, caps and uniforms were either too large or too small.

"It was," said Hutson, "the damndest parade you ever saw."

Fortunately the pair did better on the football field. But a part of the early Hutson legend doesn't involve football. He once played a varsity baseball game with his track shirt and trunks under his baseball uniform. The track adjoined the diamond. Between innings Hutson stripped and ran a 9.8 hundred.

Alabama Coach Frank Thomas used the pass sparingly and Hutson first made his name at defense. In 1932 Hutson was used so often on an end-around he was called "the fifth back." But in 1934, Howell, a so-so passer as a sophomore, was so improved by practice that the Crimson Tide began to receive attention as a passing team.

To give you an idea how times change, "the most brilliant attack Alabama has ever displayed against a major foe" was praise handed out after a 34-14 victory over Kentucky in which Howell threw nine times for 88 yards. Hutson received two and both he and Bryant scored on end-arounds.

Alabama won the Southeastern Conference title and Hutson was called by one writer "as All-American as the Star Spangled Banner." They faced a powerful Stanford team in the Rose Bowl and Howell passed himself and Hutson into football immortality after Stanford took a 7-0 lead. Seconds before the half Howell left exhausted. It was his replacement, Joe Smith, who called a pass. The call was desperation—Hutson simply ran as far and as fast as he could. Smith put the ball up and Hutson took it for a 53-yard touchdown.

Howell came back after intermission, completing five of six to Hutson for 123 yards and a 59-yard touchdown, as Alabama won 29-13. That was a massive air attack in those days.

Hutson's reputation preceded him to Green Bay, but he improved on it. He faced the Packers' traditional rival in his first pro game. Beattie Feathers, a great Bear halfback, was assigned to guard him in those single-platoon days of the complete football player.

Hutson loped down the field. So did Johnny Blood, then the Packer's leading receiver. Feathers turned to look at Blood for an instant. Hutson was gone. Arnie Herber whipped the ball to him for an 80-yard touchdown, the only score of the game.

Hutson played defensive end. He was beating himself into the ground against bigger linemen and might have had to shorten his career except that Larry Craig, a blocking back from South Carolina, came along. Craig moved in at Hutson's end and Don retired to the comparative shelter of safety.

He caught them long or short. With the ball on the two-yard line in the 1939 Pro Bowl game, Hutson took off. Isbell, who had replaced the strong-armed Herber, put the ball 69 yards in the air. Hutson went all the way—the play covering 108 yards.

On October 8, 1942 Green Bay was rolling over the Cleveland Rams. The ball was on Cleveland's four-inch line, first down. Isbell passed to Hutson. The ball almost went over his head, but Hutson leaped and brought it in for a touchdown. "Don't ever do that again," pleaded Coach Curly Lambeau.

Hutson's salary was regarded as so immense by management that it paid him with two weekly pay checks—three hundred dollars a game. "I loved football," he said, "but all my life I wanted to be in business for myself, and I used football toward that goal," By the time he stepped down he was set for successful automobile franchises, first in Green Bay, then in Racine. He was frequently too busy to get to Packer games, but little matter—he left behind the reputation against which all other pass receivers would be measured. He remains, for all time, *the* end.

Nonpareil though Hutson was, he did not stand alone at his position, even during his playing days. Wayne Millner was moving toward the Hall of Fame, receiving Sammy Baugh's passes. And there was a tremendous end for the Chicago Bears named Bill Hewitt, who insisted on playing without a helmet—until the league forced him to wear one—much as Layne, decades later, was the only player in the NFL to operate without a face mask.

The bare head symbolized Hewitt's independence and ruggedness from the day he joined Chicago out of Michigan in 1932. He was called "Offsides" Hewitt for his practice of lining up a couple of yards behind the line of scrimmage, uncannily anticipating the count with a rush that brought him to scrimmage just as the ball was snapped and, if he guessed right, into the backfield before the play developed. On such occasions he frequently dropped the ball carrier for major losses. When he guessed wrong—a five yard penalty. A murderous tackler, he was capable of winning the game by himself. When the Bears trailed the Packers in a season's opener, he roared back with an end-around, throwing a pass on the dead run to Luke Johnson for a score that tied the game. Then, as Green Bay attempted a punt, Hewitt crashed through, blocked it and carried the ball over for the winning touchdown.

Hewitt, who died in an automobile accident in 1947, typified the often erratic behavior of the end who must learn to catch a ball with a "fearless disregard of the consequences," in Red Hickey's phrase. None did so better than Elroy Hirsch, called "Crazylegs," of whom Van Brocklin said, "He could bend his head back in full flight to catch a pass. He was not a faker, but he didn't have to fool 'em. They had to respect his speed and play him deep, and when he put on the brakes for a hook pass, he was wide open."

Hirsch was born in the northern Wisconsin town of Wausau, of Norwegian-German parentage. He seemed only an average high school player, performing on the "B" team in his sophomore year, when he suddenly caught fire, picking up 270 yards as a halfback in a single game. He went on to captain the football team and win letters in basketball and baseball.

Elroy Hirsch exemplified the dictum that ends must play with a fearless disregard of the consequences. He was able to catch passes while running at full speed with his head turned back.

As a 19-year-old at the University of Wisconsin he achieved All-American rating, gaining 786 yards on 141 carried for a 5.4 average, passing 18 times for 226 yards and three touchdowns, catching one pass for 16 yards, scoring five touchdowns on the ground, punting four times for a 48.8-yard average, intercepting six passes, returning six kickoffs for 129 yards and 15 punts for 182 yards.

When he got off a long run in a 1942 upset of a favored Great Lakes team, a Chicago sportswriter noted that everyone had a shot at him but none could tackle him "because of his crazy legs." The nickname stuck. Asked if it bothered him, Hirsch said, "It's better than 'Elroy.'"

Along with others on an outstanding Badger team, he was transferred under the wartime naval V-12 program in what was called "Wisconsin's lend-lease to Michigan." There he became the first man ever to win four letters in one year, duplicating a Hutson-like feat by taking the broad jump in a triangular meet, then moving over to pitch a 5-0 shutout of Ohio State in baseball.

The same backfield coach who coached Tom Harmon called Hirsch "the greatest halfback I've ever seen" and Bennie Oosterbaan, later head football coach at Michigan, said he was "the greatest competitor I ever saw." He was capable of going out for a sport as the only means of getting back to Madison to see his high school sweetheart, the minister's daughter he subsequently married.

The 1944 All-Stars beat the Rams 16-0 when Hirsch scored on a 60-yard pass play, then picked up a touchdown on an end-around behind a block by Pat Harder, his former Wisconsin teammate, that nearly broke Hickey in two.

He turned pro after the war, joining the Chicago Rockets of the All-American Conference, a team so inept as to be called "the Rockettes." In 1948 he failed to get up from under a pile of Cleveland Browns. He was taken from the lineup. Two days later, as he lay dizzily on the couch at home, he received a call from a doctor who had just looked over the X-rays. His skull was fractured he was told, and the doctor advised him not to move. It was the medical opinion that he could never play football again.

But Hirsch secretly went to the high school gym to work out privately. There were blackouts, times when he fell on his face with no memory of what happened. But a year later he signed with the Rams where he was moved to an end post in the three-end offense that revolutionized the sport.

The frequent target of passes from both Waterfield and Van Brocklin, Hirsch went on to tie Hutson's season record of 17 touchdown passes and broke his yards-gained mark with 1,495. When the Rams trailed the 49ers 16-13 in the final quarter, Waterfield went deep, throwing 45 yards to Hirsch who caught the ball with two defenders hanging on him, broke away and scored.

"People tend to think of us professionals as guys who spend all their time around the swimming pool with a blonde in one hand and a martini in the other," said Hirsch. "They don't realize that a lot of us don't like martinis."

Facing the very physical Philadelphia team, Hirsch went around to the rookies in the Los Angeles dressing room telling them, "Look out for Kilroy, number 76. He'll kill you if you don't watch out." "Remember 76. Kilroy." "76. He's likely to try to flatten you." There was a pass interception in the final quarter. "I was standing there, trying to figure out what happened when I got a bang on the side of my head that stretched me. I looked up, and there was Kilroy, grinning."

As is the case with most players, Hirsch found he was ready to retire when "it was no longer fun. I didn't mind the games so much, but I hated practice." After his final game fans poured out on the field and stripped him of all but his shorts and ankle bandages.

He made some movies, a critic calling his performance "as sincere as a punch in the nose." In one, he worked with the inmates at Chino Correctional Institution, showing them how to play football. They came to him with a trick formation using 12 men. "Only 11 men to a side," he said. "That's why we're in prison," said one. "We don't obey the rules."

Hirsch became general manager of the Rams, the only thing both sides could agree on during the ownership disputes of the early sixties. He left to become athletic director at the University of Wisconsin whose football teams had fallen on dismal days. "I didn't leave California," he promised, "to come out here and freeze my fanny off with a loser."

Like Hirsch, Pete Pihos came to the Hall from the Big Ten where he starred at two positions. He was an All-American end at the University of Indiana before World War II interrupted his career. He won four battle stars and a battlefield commission, but when he came back, All-American Bob Ravernsburg was settled in at his post with the other end slot occupied by Ted Kluszewski who would go on to become one of the National League's most powerful sluggers as a Cincinnati Red. So Pihos shifted to fullback.

He returned to the end position for nine memorable years with the Philadelphia Eagles, twice as they won NFL championships. Those were the Eagle teams of Steve Van Buren and quarterback Tommy Thompson. A short pass behind the line became "the Pihos screen" and ripped enemy defenses. He scored one of the two Eagle touchdowns in the championship victory over Los Angeles in which Van Buren ran wild, taking a 31-yard pass from Thompson. Six times Pihos was named All-Pro, catching 373 passes for 63 touchdowns and 5,169 yards. League honors came to him both as an offensive and defensive end. Once against the then Chicago Cardinals, he fell on an enemy fumble, got up and raced for a score, then fell on another fumble which led to the game-winning field goal. It was said that the Bears staved him off in his final appearance, Chicago winning 17-10. All he did that day in 1955 was catch 11 passes for 114 yards.

The offensive statistics for the other end in the Hall of Fame are just about zero. Andy Robustelli's presence indicates changes in both the game and in fans' interests. When the New York Giants shut out the Cleveland Browns, holding the great Jim Brown to just 16 yards rushing, delirious fans broke from the stands to carry their heroes off the field: Robustelli and middle linebacker Sam Huff. The offensive stars walked off not quite ignored.

"It's a long way to come," said Robustelli when he was inducted into the Hall, "for a little Italian kid who loved to go to the store for his mother to buy Italian bread shaped like a football, so he could run home saying, 'That's Robustelli on the 50, the 40, the 30.' When I scored, I was home."

A native of Stamford, Connecticut, he attended little Arnold College. The New York Yankees scouted him, determining that he was "good hit, no field." "When you can't do anything about it," Robustelli said, speaking a philosophic truth, "you shouldn't waste time in vain regrets. But the day I was scouted, I was shifted from my position as catcher to third base in an emergency. I fielded balls with my chest rather than let them go through."

He was drafted nineteenth by the Los Angeles Rams. He also had a teaching offer for $2,400 a year. He asked his Stamford

Andy Robustelli held down an end post and captained the greatest of all New York Giant teams in an era when professional football reached its present, exalted status. The Robustelli defense drew more crowds than the biggest smash-hit Broadway play.

friend Walter Kennedy, commissioner of the National Basketball Association, what he should do. Kennedy advised him to take the teaching job, saying football could give him neither the money nor the security. But after talking it over with his wife, Robustelli decided "I could never forgive myself if I didn't try" and made the long trip across the nation. He nearly turned around and came back. The Ram receivers included Hirsch, Fears and Bob Boyd. Providentially, Jack Zilly tore a muscle and Robustelli got a shot on defense.

"A guy played because he loved the game," Robustelli recalled. "If a kid was lucky enough to get a bonus, it was a small one. Nobody even thought about a pension plan. Players got nothing for a pre-season game then, and once the Rams drew 90,000 for an exhibition. Most guys played six years and got out. There was no point in staying on."

Robustelli stayed on to make All-Pro eight times in a 13-year career which almost ended before it began. San Francisco's Frankie Albert suckered Robustelli three times on a bootleg; Hirsch saved the game with an acrobatic catch in the end zone. Robustelli learned.

Tittle recalled later leading the 49ers against the Rams, "I cocked my arm to throw for what would have been the winning touchdown. Andy suddenly ducked through from nowhere, grabbed the ball and went in to score."

All that sun apparently induces West Coast owners into disadvantageous trades. Robustelli came to the New York Giants in the middle 1950s and settled down with Jim Katcavage, Ed Modzelewski and Rosey Grier as a front four that diverted fans' interest to the defense and dominated the Eastern Conference through the rest of the decade and on into the 1960s.

Arming themselves with coolers of beer and stacks of bologna sandwiches, the clientele packed Yankee Stadium. When the defense took over there developed an eerie cheer modeled after the middle linebacker's last name. "Huff, huff, huff, huff," steamed the voices. The Giants on offense—ignited by Tittle in from San Francisco—were just about treated as intermissions. With the stadium sold out and the ban on home television, the hearty simply took over motels outside the 75-mile blackout area for the afternoon, catching the game on television. Some motel proprietors furnished half time shows on the parking lot.

Soon it became necessary for other teams to honor their defenses. Dallas came up with a Doomsday Defense, Los Angeles with the Fearsome Foursome, Minnesota with the Purple People-Eaters. It was all for the good of the game. Rooting for your favorite team no longer required its possession of the ball; it became a 60-minute occupation.

When the high-powered Giant offense slowed down, the defense took up the slack. "It got pretty bad," Kyle Rote recalled. "I remember going out on the field to take over on offense after the defense scored on the Cardinals. Robustelli was coming off, and he stopped to pat me on the back. 'See if you can hold them,' he said."

Individual defensive statistics, once the province of the coaching staff, became part of the fans' intellectual luggage. In the 1956 title game Chicago's outstanding ball carrier Rick Casares was held to 11 yards in 12 carries. Huff made ten individual tackles. The Giants romped 43-7.

Robustelli, who owned a sporting goods store, brought in sneakers for the team after hearing weather reports of cold and ice. "We were better shod," he said. "And we were also the better team." Dominating his career statistics were 22 blocked kicks.

"He hits you so hard your bones rattle," Bobby Layne said of Robustelli. "But he's not malicious, and he always plays fair." Katcavage said, "There's never been a better pass-rusher. When you hit a good quarterback twice in one game, you're accomplishing as much as a home run in baseball. Andy hit Cleveland's George Ratterman, who was having a good season, six times." During the six years the Giant front four was intact— Robustelli played in 131 consecutive regular league games—the Giants were by far the best in the league, putting together a 51-20 record.

Not long before the years caught up to him and he retired, Robustelli was honored with the Philadelphia Touchdown Club's Maxwell Trophy as the NFL's outstanding player.

"I'd like to think I'm the best player," he said, "but I'm realistic and accept it as a consideration for the players who are not touchdown-makers. I feel fortunate to represent this kind of man."

POWER IN
THE PIT

"The greatest football players who ever lived," said Bo McMillin, who as player and coach graced the sport from early in the century until his death in 1950, "was Cal Hubbard—the greatest lineman or back, college or pro."

Robert "Cal" Hubbard at 254 pounds was not a touchdown-maker. A man-mountain for his time, he played tackle for the Giants and Packers from 1927 to 1936. He also was an American League umpire, ultimately becoming umpire-in-chief. Few baseball players argued with him.

"Big Cal was as kind and generous a man off the field as he was an untamed savage on it," said a college president who knew him. But Hubbard could be provoked. He once violated the Sabbath by knocking out an antagonist behind the church.

Chicago once determined to anger him into getting thrown out of the game. Phil Handler, a substitute guard, was given the assignment. "Get away from me small change," said Hubbard. "I'm not getting tossed out for the likes of you." But a free-for-all developed with fan participation in the Chicago-Green Bay tradition. The field eventually was cleared, but Handler lay unconscious.

"When no official was looking," said Hubbard, "I pole-axed the so-and-so."

A native of Keatesville, Missouri, a "community so small it isn't even in the big atlas," the schoolboy Hubbard worshipped Bo McMillin. McMillin brought a team to Columbia, Missouri for a track meet, met Hubbard and brought him back to Louisiana's Centenary College. Two years later player and coach moved on to Geneva College in Pennsylvania.

Hubbard's standing instructions to his quarterback were, "Look, little boy. Take the ball and follow me."

The powerful Cornell team of Gil Dobie scheduled Geneva as a breather. The Big Red won aided by 300 yards in penalties. Hubbard was convinced that Dobie was illegally sending in plays by arranging cups on the water tray. He kicked over the tray every time the water boy came on the field. A year later Harvard repeated Cornell's errors and Geneva "passed them dizzy," Hubbard recalled, winning 16-7. Harvard introduced the huddle in that game.

Not to be outdone, Hubbard decided the tackle post was too restricting. He took to roaming around behind scrimmage, inventing, some say, the position of linebacker.

He was hardly a blushing violet. Spotting a pretty coed on campus one day, he demanded, "What's your name?" "Ruth Frishkorn," she said. "That name's too hard to pronounce," he replied. "I'm going to change it to Hubbard." And he did.

Defense dominated the sport. Explained Hubbard, "Our favorite trick with Green Bay was to get possession and let Verne Lewellyn kick the opposition way back near their goal line. They'd come back if they could, but if they did we'd repeat. And after a while we had the other team plain wore out."

"Today," Hubbard continued, "if the other team scores, you know you will too, as soon as you get the ball. That's why you have NFL scores like 45-42. You can't tell me a game like that will be played if the other team has any defense."

In fact there are signs that the defense again has caught up with the offense in recent years. Owners, disturbed because they believe fans demand high-scoring games, are fooling with the rules to bring about more touchdowns. This is not a procedure likely to be looked on favorably by purists like Hubbard.

"We came back from the East with the title clinched one year," he remembered. "It made no difference who won the

Chicago game, so we decided to open up. Either we'd win by
35 points or we'd get snowed under. We scored in the first minute. . . . We missed the kick. The Bears came back and kicked
the point.

"You know what the final score was? 7-6. Both teams were
so ingrained on defense we choked each other the next 55
minutes."

Hubbard's decision to quit the game was sudden. He was
back with the Giants, playing the Boston Yankees, when Giant
halfback Les Corzine plunged into the line. There was an awful
cracking sound. Corzine's leg was broken in three places. "Suppose that were me?" asked Hubbard. Near game's end he called
time for an announcement to the opposition:

"If any of you guys has a grudge against me, get it out of
your system in the next minute and five seconds. This is your
last shot at me. Come and get me, because I'm through after
this game."

There were no takers.

Hubbard was so big for his time and so colorful that he demanded attention. But although coaches and players and knowl-
edgeable fans understood that games were won in the line, in
what is called "the battle of the pit," linemen were virtually
unnoticed. Happily that day is past. Offensive linemen are still
the lowest paid athletes in the sport, demonstrating again that
salary doesn't necessarily equal worth. But Grady Alderman,
Ralph Neely and Forrest Blue won their share of notice.

And so the Hall of Fame linemen can be seen as surrogates
for the college and high school athletes who pave the way for
the ball carrier. Sometimes recognition is given. Albert Glen
"Turk" Edwards was three times named All-American tackle at
Washington State where he captained the squad as a senior
in 1931. "A true sportsman, a true gentleman," in the words of
college teammate Mel Hein, Turk joined the Boston Redskins
and followed them to Washington, making All-Pro four times
before bad knees ended his career in 1940. *Time* magazine gave
him equal billing with the offensive stars when Washington
defeated New York in a "must" game: "Baugh completed 11 of
15 passes, Cliff Battles gained more than 200 yards and Turk
Edwards broke open the hitherto impregnable Giant line."

Named All-Pro five of his nine years with the Brooklyn Dodgers, Frank "Bruiser" Kinard impressed Coach Jock Sutherland with his intellectual appreciation of football.

So it was with Frank "Bruiser" Kinard, six-one and 212 pounds in college, called "the greatest tackle who ever lived" at the University of Mississippi and "Ole Miss' greatest athlete." When he broke a bone in his ankle he wrapped it in tape and played on, averaging better than 55 minutes a game through three seasons, including one 562-minute stretch. He was named All-Pro five times in a nine-year career with the Brooklyn Dodgers. Jock Sutherland, his coach at Brooklyn, said "He took his football seriously. He got so much more out of it than many players because he enjoyed the intellectual aspects of the game. Bruiser

In 14 years with the Pittsburgh Steelers, Ernie Stautner played in the Pro Bowl eight times, but never realized his ambition of playing with a championship team.

was a great competitor and a great tackle."

But fate deals out its rewards unevenly. When Ernie Stautner and Art Donovan played for Boston College, Stautner so dominated the line that Donovan was called "the other tackle." Stautner played in the Pro Bowl eight times. Donovan was All-Pro five times.

Stautner said, "I want so badly to play on a championship team. I've been saying that so long I've given up talking about it." In 14 years with the Pittsburgh Steelers Stautner never knew that thrill.

Donovan, on the other hand, joined the failing Baltimore Colt franchise, moved on to Cleveland where he was cut for a man who could play both ways, then rejoined the Colts where he starred on the championship teams of 1958-1959.

"A giant of a man in character as well as physique," wrote John Steadman of the *Baltimore News-American* the day Donovan retired. "He is more than a football player, he is an institution—Santa Claus in helmet and pads. Few men ever put more into the game. He is indisputable proof again that living the good life, being kind to fellow travelers in a world smeared with selfishness and greed does indeed bring great rewards."

The gentleness was not reflected on the field. Doubtful of his spirit, the Colts matched the rookie Donovan with a highly-touted lineman from the Southwest Conference. Donovan dismembered him.

"He is a tremendously powerful man," said Red Hickey. "He likes to have a blocker come in on him so he can get his hands on him and throw him wherever he wants to. We knew that when we played the Colts, so we told the guard who was blocking him to stay away from him. This guard danced around in front of Donovan all afternoon, staying in his way but never getting close enough for Donovan to get hold of him.

"Finally he started yelling at the guard, 'Come on, you so-and-so. Come on in to me.' But he never did get around the kid to reach our passer, and we beat the Colts. But Donovan is a great tackle because he's a mean tackle."

Donovan's greatest problem, however, was his weight.

"Weeb Ewbank had a clause in my contract that if I could get through the season never weighing more than 270, I'd get a $1,000 bonus. He would weigh me unexpectedly every now and then, and I always got by except one time. It was late in 1959 when we were just about to win the championship. I got on the scales for Weeb and I weighed 271. That cost me $1,000."

The reason was obvious. "I like pizza, hamburgers and hot dogs," Donovan said. "I eat hot dogs the way you do peanuts. I ate 25 of them one night at a barbecue without much trouble. They didn't do me any harm." But he once ballooned to 315 pounds.

The Colts offered a horrible example in Sherman Plunkett, who later ate his way out of work with the New York Jets. "We could tell how much he weighed by the wrinkles in his neck," said Donovan. "If he had three wrinkles, he weighed 320. Four, and he weighed 360."

Donovan's specialty was making things tough for the back who pretended to have the ball when he didn't. After a period of being worked over on decoy assignment, "they made sure Donovan knew they didn't have the ball," said an observer, citing Donovan as "a man who roughs up players by calculation and with a definite purpose but never intentionally injures anyone."

He was ill with tension before every game. "Don't you get sick on me," warned an opposing player who found Donovan green around the gills. "I loved to play football," said Donovan. "In the pros, I think everyone does. If you didn't, you couldn't survive. You didn't mention your injuries. You played with your injuries."

His old college teammate Stautner echoed the sentiments. "If you don't like contact, you don't like football. The major part of this game is hit."

Unlike Donovan, Stautner's problem was lack of size. Six-two and listed at 230, "I was one of the smallest linemen in the league, and I would be much too small to be considered today. I developed a good, hard arm charge and used my hands a great deal. I got off the ball fast. I see linemen today who are fast but don't get off fast at the snap. They are keying on their opponents' moves but not on the ball. That gives the opponents the initiative."

Gruff-voiced and pugnacious, Stautner was an intelligent man. He filled many roles for the Steelers. "The only way to make the pros respect you" goes a piece of foolish advice, "is to pick the toughest guy on the team and lick him." Invariably rookies picked Stautner. Invariably Stautner cleaned their clocks.

He remained an eternal sophomore after 14 seasons in the league. When he was named to the Hall of Fame he said, "Three distinctive events in my life stand out. When my parents chose to move the family from Germany to this country. When

I was first involved in football on the sandlots of Albany, New York, and the game became a motivating force. And now, this occasion."

Joe Stydahar came from a more rugged tradition. As a Bear, he once hit an opposing lineman so hard the fellow's arm split open. Officials thought Stydahar bit him. They examined his mouth and found no teeth. He had lost his own as an All-American tackle at West Virginia in 1935. Another time, upset when a 225-pound opponent mauled Chicago back Hugh Gallernau, Stydahar picked him up and held him at arm's length off the ground. "Now, cut that out," he warned sternly. "Yes, sir," said the offender.

The Chicago spirit of the time infected their crosstown rivals, the Cardinals. Pat Harder, feeling he had been roughed up on a point-after attempt by Cleveland's vast Len Ford, took the following revenge on a simple one-play blocking assignment —he sent Ford to the hospital with a broken forehead bone, broken cheekbone, broken jaw and broken nose. *Ford* drew a 15-yard penalty on the play.

Stydahar, six-four and 240 pounds, starred on the Bear championship teams of 1940 and 1941. When he succeeded Shaughnessy as Ram coach in 1950, Shaughnessy called a press conference to make his celebrated crack that he could coach a high school team to victory over a Stydahar squad.

But "Jumbo Joe," as he was called in his playing days, was not without resources of his own. After San Francisco stopped the passing of Van Brocklin and Waterfield with a covey of light defensive players, Stydahar opened the rematch with a bull elephant backfield. Dick Hoerner, 220, Tank Younger, 226, and Deacon Dan Towler, 222, trod roughly on the lighter 49ers. San Francisco substituted heavier men and was shortly passed to death.

"After you throw the ball, don't stand there and watch its gentle flight," Stydahar once warned Van Brocklin. "Find cover." Van Brocklin ignored his advice, throwing the ball and waiting to see if it was caught. He got four broken ribs.

The Rams tied Chicago for the conference title, won a playoff and then lost to Cleveland in the last 38 seconds. The following year they won the division title. On the final day when they

Toothless Joe Stydahar once belted a foe so hard that officials thought he bit him until examination of Stydahar's mouth proved this an impossibility. But even as coach Stydahar regarded possession of teeth an insult to the spirit of the game.

defeated Green Bay, the Cardinals beat the Bears and San Francisco upset Detroit. (Ram owner Dan Reeves telephoned 49er President Tony Morabito to say, "If you come to my house, you can have anything you want.") But after the Rams lost four in a row in 1952, Stydahar was deposed. He returned to coach the Cardinals through two disastrous seasons and then retired from the sport.

If Stydahar wore his battle scars proudly, Leo Nomellini proved it didn't have to be that way. In 14 violent seasons with the 49ers, the 255-pound Hall of Fame tackle suffered no more than a broken thumb and forefinger and the loss of two front teeth. He played in a record 174 consecutive regular season games and was named to ten Pro Bowl contests.

Amazingly, Nomellini never played football until he served in the Marine Corps during World War II. He was born in Lucca, Italy, coming to this country when he was a year old. He grew up on Chicago's rugged northwest side. There was no time for sport. He sold newspapers after school, then worked in a foundry before graduating from vocational school.

He was invited to try out for a service squad and fell in love with the sport, even as he did with wrestling, another activity he discovered in the Marines. After seeing combat on Okinawa he was discharged. He sought out a college with no success until he was interviewed by Bernie Bierman at the University of Minnesota. Bierman was one of the great college coaches whose teams tyrannized the nation during the 1930s.

He took a chance on Nomellini who started in the first college game he ever saw, won Big Ten and All-American honors and became Minnesota's greatest tackle since his idol Bronk Nagurski. He also won the Big Ten heavyweight wrestling championship.

As a 49er rookie he suffered the indignity of being knocked out by one of the smallest men in the game, Buddy Young, when he stooped over to scoop up a fumble. But he recovered after a few minutes on the sideline and went on to compile his astonishing endurance mark.

He was quickly recognized as one of the pro sport's outstanding lineman, unmovable and even stronger than other men his size. He was named to the All-Pro squad six times. "No two men can handle him when he's aroused," went the observation. He took apart the Chicago Cardinals after Coach Frankie Albert motivated him with the false story that the Cardinals planned to draft him, then drop him after capitalizing on his appeal in the Midwest during the exhibition season.

Although he played both ways, he preferred defense because "when an opponent tries to block me" he said, "he has to make the first move, and I have a better chance to counter it."

Nomellini wrestled professionally during the off season, becoming the West Coast's biggest drawing card. He said the sport

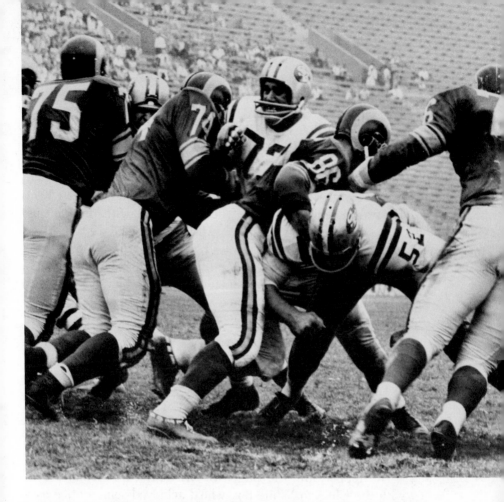

Leo Nomellini learned football in the Marine Corps and went on to prove with the San Francisco 49ers that a service-acquired skill can be of lasting worth in civilian life. Once aroused, Nomellini could handle a platoon of enemy blockers.

"put at least five years on my career, improved my footwork and the moves I learned helped keep me from getting hurt in football."

Once he teamed with his old idol Nagurski in tag team matches. He sent Nagurski an old suit and offered him more, but Bronko wrote him, "Thanks for the suit. But it's too small in the shoulders and too big in the seat." The 49ers called in a team of psychologists to determine the mental makeup of the squad. End Monty Stickles wondered, "What if they find out after 14 years that Nomellini's chicken?"

It was only a joke. As Hickey said, "Nomellini is living proof that it pays to stay in shape all year round."

Of all the line positions, however, none is more important than center. The Hall of Heroes honors five men who get play under way by snapping the ball, and if Mel Hein is the consensus choice for all-time honors, the others are not far behind. Take George Trafton, for example, who died at age 74 in 1971. He was called "the Brute" when he played with the Chicago Bears, eight of the years as an All-Pro. "I spilled a lot of blood in my day," he said, "and it wasn't all mine."

Bounced from Notre Dame by no less than Knute Rockne who discovered he was playing semi-pro ball on Sundays, Trafton quickly found a home with the Bears. He became annoyed at a Cardinal player who worked him over with forearm shots.

"That's called the Southern California armblock," he was told. "Don't you like it?"

Trafton prevailed on a couple of teammates to pin his antagonist in place by stepping on his feet. Trafton then backed off and ran up the fellow's features.

"That," he said cheerfully, "is called the Notre Dame drop kick. Don't you like it?"

He stepped into the ring with Art Shires, a baseball player with the Chicago White Sox who'd achieved some notice as a boxer. Trafton took care of him with a first round knockout, "picking up a couple of thousand bucks, which wasn't bad in those days."

He sometimes centered the ball and then fell flat on his stomach to watch the play develop. Trafton claimed, "You could really find action on defense. That I loved."

He became the sport's first roving center, moving about behind scrimmage on defense. And he was heady. He crashed through to block a Green Bay punt but gave the credit to "that kid," end Hewitt. On the next punting situation the Packers massed to block Hewitt. In came Trafton again to block the kick in a 19-14 victory.

After his departure the Bears experimented with a number of centers until another All-Pro came along to play his way into the Hall of Fame. But Clyde "Bulldog" Turner, who starred

In an attempt to find a college that would take him, Clyde "Bulldog" Turner hitch-hiked without food or drink for days on end. Tough luck for those schools that turned him down because Turner became center for the greatest one-platoon team—the Chicago Bears of the early 1940s.

from 1940 through 1952, was worth waiting for. He grew up on a west Texas ranch. He quit picking cotton after school to try out for the football team so he could win a letter sweater. "I found something I didn't anticipate. I found I loved to play football," he said.

Like Nomellini, he sought out a college. But there were no takers during those depression days and he returned after five days and five nights hitch hiking without food. "My ma started crying. I had lost a lot of weight and my eyes were sunk back."

He finally enrolled at Hardin-Simmons and won wide recognition in a defeat of Loyola of Los Angeles. The Bears and Lions squabbled over him and Bulldog chose Chicago.

"I feared no man," he said. Things weren't quite as tough around the league as they had been in Trafton's day. "On the team I was with you got an automatic $100 fine for fighting. Then the league hit you for $50 if you were thrown out of the game. A lot of the guys weren't making more than $150 a game."

But it was bad enough. Five times Turner's nose was broken by a 300-pound middle guard for the Packers named Ed Neale, who used to warm up for the game by breaking beer bottles across his forearm. "His arms were big as my leg," Turner recalled. Neale used to charge over Turner whenever Luckman went back to pass. Turner suggested Luckman slip the ball to the fullback "and let him come right up here, 'cause there's nobody here but me." That, Turner claimed, was the invention of the draw play, and Chicago averaged 33 yards with it the following year.

Years after Turner retired he came back to coach the Titans, the ill-fated predecessors of the New York Jets. But he devoted most of his time to breeding quarter horses in Texas. "I believe you will find that horses give you better effort every day than people," he said. "They've got great heart."

So did Turner's great rival Alex Wojciechowicz, for 13 years the typesetter's nightmare as he starred with Detroit and Philadelphia. He was one of Fordham's famed Seven Blocks of Granite, playing shoulder-to-shoulder with Vince Lombardi on a team that won football immortality by shutting out Southern Methodist, Pittsburgh and St. Mary's. His coach Jim Crowley, who advised him against changing his name "because nobody can overlook it," called him the greatest college lineman he ever saw, and the pros never questioned that judgment.

Hall of Fame centers seem to run almost consecutively on teams. Wojie was succeeded at Philadelphia by Chuck Bednarik, All-Pro eight times in his 14-year career. He would be remembered, if for nothing else than for the play that nearly ended the career of Frank Gifford, one of the Giants' glamour backs.

The teams were fighting for the Eastern Division title in 1960. Philadelphia led late in the game when New York moved into

Eagle territory. Cutting across the middle, Gifford caught a pass from George Shaw. He saw Bednarik moving at him from his middle linebacker position, then took his eyes from him to deal with Don Burroughs in the secondary.

Bednarik hit him from the blind side, sticking a shoulder into his chest and coming up to his chin. Gifford fell, dropping the ball. Eagle Chuck Weber recovered it. Bednarik, an emotional man, did a victory dance, crying, "We got it! We got it! That's the ball game."

But the Giants thought he danced over the motionless Gifford. Charlie Conerly called him "a cheap shot artist." Gifford, unconscious, was taken from the game with a deep concussion and transferred to a hospital, after which doctors advised him against playing again. After sitting out a season he came back to play, but Bednarik, who considered him "the best halfback I ever faced," never got over the Giants' accusations.

"I don't play dirty," he said. "You'd have to be crazy to deliberately hurt a guy in this game." Gifford himself absolved Bednarik, saying it was a clean tackle. But eyes were still on Bednarik when he inactivated Paul Hornung in the title game against Green Bay later that season.

He had noticed in game films that Hornung liked to cut back while running a wide sweep. The Packers were driving in Eagle territory when Starr called the play. Bednarik diagnosed it, sticking a shoulder under Hornung's arm and pinching a nerve in his neck. Hornung came back for only a few plays after that and Philadelphia took the championship.

Bednarik formed a "life is tough" philosophy early. His father was a Czech immigrant who worked in the steel mills of Bethlehem, Pennsylvania. Young Chuck spent just enough time in them to learn "they're not a boys' camp." He played football, basketball and baseball in high school then flew 30 missions as a waist gunner over Germany in World War II.

At the University of Pennsylvania he won All-American honors, doubling as the team's punter. He became the first lineman to win the Maxwell Award. Like Nomellini, he played both ways until he moved to the defense late in his professional career. He was nicknamed "the Clutch" for his ability to hold ball carriers and receivers at the line of scrimmage.

`Oddly, the Eagles trailed the Giants in the game in which Gifford was hurt until Bednarik came in at offensive center. Then things started falling in place. It was that way through his storied, hard-bitten career. He was a tremendous competitor.

The football years were running out on him when he was dropped early in a game against Cleveland. Coach Paul Brown, making a rare error, taunted him. "You're getting too old for this game," he teased.

Furious, Bednarik pulled himself to his feet and played wildly for 59 minutes. The Eagles won on a field goal by Bobby Walston in the closing seconds, 31-29.

Bednarik retired to a line of work some found appropriate—cement salesman. But the man who once called Sam Huff "an overrated hillbilly who never wore shoes until he got to New York," lost none of his fire. Years after he retired he said, "Joe Namath is one of the all-time greats, but in person I think he'a a real creep. Because of him, we have too many longhairs in football. Long hair and football don't mix." After Dallas' Duane Thomas threatened to sit out the season unless his contract was readjusted, Bednarik said, "He thinks he's All-World. I hope he never plays again."

Looking back on a career which saw him against the very best, he had no doubts about one thing:

"Jim Brown is the toughest back I've ever banged up against."

9

But is the backs who advance the ball and score the points and attract the most attention. The backs whose skills are most highly visible. The backs who are out there in the open or crashing through the line like thunder, breaking tackle and stride and the hearts of fans, taking down the most money, the most acclaim, the most attention.

Even little boys who grow up to be great defensive ends or centers or coaches and know all about the battle of the pit, even they start out in young dreams carrying the leather for immortality. It is the backs whose chapters are written in flaming letters.

You can get an argument on just about anything in professional football, and it's always safe to dodge the questions by saying you can't compare the oldtimers with the modern players because the game has changed. But of the backs, most agree the greatest was Jimmy Brown. Just look at the records . . . and the films . . . and the newspaper and magazine accounts.

Not that any of the backs in the Hall of Fame are there on sufferance. Each earned his niche, his chunk of football immortality. Take Thorpe's old teammate with the Canton Bulldogs, Indian Joe Guyon. A great newspaperman named Ralph McGill, who wrote for the *Atlanta Constitution,* looked back to say:

"There is no doubt about the identity of the greatest football player who ever performed in Dixie. There is a grand argument about second place, but for first place there is Joe Guyon, the Chippewa brave." Guyon went from Carlisle, which was really a vocational school, to Georgia Tech, playing on the team that ran up college football's highest score—220-0 over Cumberland. It is little wonder that McGill was impressed. Playing against the Staleys, Guyon one day noticed George Halas moving in to hit him, as Halas thought, from the blind side. Guyon waited until the last second then spun around and kneed Halas, breaking three of his ribs. "What the hell, Halas," Guyon said as they carted the great man off, "don't you know you can't sneak up on an Indian?"

Incredible though it was, Ernie Nevers' feat of averaging a game every four days his first year as a professional was by no means his only storied performance. The man Pop Warner thought was better than Thorpe put together the kind of career you find only in story books. As an instance of his versatility, he played against Grange, Thorpe and Nagurski in football, against Babe Ruth and Ty Cobb and Tris Speaker in baseball, each among the greatest his sport ever produced. Nevers remembers with mixed feelings that as a pitcher for the St. Louis Browns he threw two home run balls to Ruth the year that Ruth hit his record total of 60.

Minnesota-born, Nevers went to high school in Superior, Wisconsin before his family moved to California. Stanford's greatest athlete, he was a powerful line plunger who ran over people, a first-rate blocker, tackler, top passer and punter. He broke his left ankle in a September scrimmage his senior year and sat out most of the season. Coming in for the next-to-last game, he broke his right ankle. Bone specialists couldn't figure out a method, so Warner devised a brace that kept Nevers on his feet. He walked through the plays in scrimmage.

Then, against Notre Dame's Four Horsemen in the Rose Bowl, playing on those damaged legs, he carried the ball 34 times, made four of five tackles through 60 minutes, intercepted a pass and nearly outgained the entire Irish backfield. Still Stanford lost 24-10. His teammates had to lift him to his feet after some of his efforts, but he never quit battering at the line.

He received $25,000 to lead a team against Grange for one

When All-American Ernie Nevers left Stanford there seemed few fields left for him to conquer. But he chalked up records with the Duluth Eskimos in the rugged early days of pro football, as well as making a contribution to baseball history.

game, and signed with an old high school pal, Ole Haugsrud— 40 years later a stockholder in the Minnesota Vikings—to play with the Duluth Eskimos. "About turning pro," said Nevers, "that wasn't done in those days. I needed the money. I know this sounds corny, but I wanted to pay off the mortgage on my father's ranch."

The two-time All-American carried on with the pros as he had in college. Stricken with appendicitis four days before a game with Green Bay, he came off the bench to throw a then record 62-yard touchdown pass and kick the extra point in a 7-6 win.

(Today, of course, the conscientious coach would not allow an athlete to compete with broken bones or a physical ailment as serious as appendicitis. Oldtimers who "played hurt" frequently wound up crippled to one degree or another. On the other hand, performances like Nevers' demonstrates the high threshold of pain common to many athletes. Whether it is natural or developed, many simply do not feel pain as we do. Doctors who treat professional athletes frequently comment on this.)

But it was with the Chicago Cardinals in 1929 that Nevers realized a day uncommon even for him and set a record that has never been equaled. Playing against their bitter crosstown rivals the Bears, he scored six touchdowns and kicked four extra points, accounting for all this team's scores in a 40-6 victory. It was, he said, his proudest moment, even surpassing the day he completed 17 of 17 passes against Pottsville.

Grange, of course, deserves his place in the Hall of Fame just for stepping on the field. The crosscountry sweep he made with the Bears, while it enriched him, gave the National Football League its first prominence on the sports pages. No football player in history so completely captured the imagination of sports fans as the man who scored 31 touchdowns for Illinois. Bob Zuppke said, "He was the smoothest-running performer who ever carried the ball. He ran with rhythm, every movement of his body having meaning." The coach scrapped the T and installed what he called "the Grange formation," putting his star five-and-a-half yards behind center, giving his blockers time so that Grange would not run into them.

But there are a couple of ironies to the Grange story. The first is that it was learned he had a heart murmur when he was eight years old. Doctors said he must never engage in strenuous sports. The murmur cleared up by the time he was in high school, proving that sometimes doctors guess wrong.

The second irony is that Grange was at his peak only briefly as a professional. After his initial season with the Bears, Grange jumped to an outlaw league formed by his personal manager after Halas refused to agree to patently excessive terms for Grange's service. The next year he appeared against his old team and was tackled hard by George Trafton just as his cleats caught in the turf while he was attempting a cut.

The damage to his knee kept him out of the game for a year and robbed him of the breakaway speed and change of direction that marked his style. He remained a tough defensive player and pass receiver but as a runner, "I was just another halfback after that," he said. Like any truly great runner, he recognized the keys to his success. "I was always sorry the other ten guys on the team couldn't make All-American," he said. "I always gave credit to the blockers. They're the guys who make you look good."

Among Grange's rivals was John Victor McNally, who played 22 seasons with the Green Bay Packers and four other teams in the NFL. If that name doesn't ring a bell to fathers and grandfathers, try "Johnny Blood," the pseudonym he made famous. Of all Hall of Fame players he is perhaps the one surrounded with the greatest air of mystery, as befits a man who graduated from high school at 14 and from college at 46. There are so many stories and so many legends about Johnny Blood that the first thing to get straight is the record—he scored 224 points and 37 touchdowns in his career. He was fast, powerful enough to knock a man over, and a tremendous receiver, believing, said a teammate, that he could catch any ball thrown at him no matter the company.

He was called "the Vagabond Halfback." He spent off-seasons back in the 1920s and thirties traveling around the country, working as a seaman, a farmhand, a miner, as a stickman in a gambling house, a bartender, a hotel desk clerk, author of an unpublished book on economics called *Spend Yourself Rich,* a pick-and-shovel worker. His main concerns when he wasn't playing football were women, drink and, he said, meditating. He could hold his own in streetcorner soapbox discussions on all subjects, but he also enjoyed simply wandering, working for his keep, checking on points of interest, watching the seasons change. He played a team sport very well, but he was very much an individual.

McNally was born to a highly respectable family in New Richmond, Wisconsin. His mother, a former schoolteacher, pushed him in his studies and he was out of high school early, too skinny to have played any organized sports. He spent a year at home learning to type and studying, and then went to St. John's College, then a two-year institution in Minnesota.

So many legends surround John Victor "Johnny Blood" McNally that it's easy to forget he was a swift and slashing runner who hit with enough power to drop a tackler in his tracks.

Always wiry and fast, with a love of climbing, he filled out enough to become the school's first four-letter winner. He went to Notre Dame where the Four Horsemen seemed to take care of any backfield needs, but was dismissed from college for violating a campus curfew.

He went to work for his uncle's newspaper, *The Minneapolis Tribune*, in a technical department. Together with a former teammate he learned that a professional football team was being organized in a city league. Both he and his teammate had a year of college eligibility left and decided not to play under their true names, a common practice in those days. On the way to the practice field they passed a movie marquee advertising "Blood and Sand." McNally became "Blood," his friend, "Sand."

McNally was good enough to star for the team and good enough to play for the Packers the following year. Coach Curly Lambeau stretched his patience as far as it would go, attempting to live with a man whose legends off the field rivaled his prowess on it. As an example, Blood once won $20 by outrunning a German police dog. "It was easy," he said. "I knew the dog wasn't trained to race."

One method Lambeau used to discipline Blood was to keep him on the bench. The fans would demand he be allowed to play. Finally, when the situation was desperate for the Packers, Lambeau would relent. And that was how Blood, a man of tremendous self-confidence, won his undying reputation as a clutch player.

In 1937 Lambeau, out of patience at last, traded Blood to Pittsburgh where he became playing coach. He returned the opening kickoff of the season 100 yards for a touchdown. "That's the way to do it, fellows," he told his players. The Steelers soon won a reputation as the only team in the league where the practice was held up while the players waited for the coach to appear. One of them was Byron "Whizzer" White, an All-American from Colorado who was also a Rhodes scholar with no intention of playing professional football. Blood talked him into it and the men became fast friends. White was a great football player, but he is best known today as an associate justice of the United States Supreme Court.

"Coaching the Steelers and playing 60 minutes," said Blood, "I was making $2,500. Whizzer White, my halfback, was making $17,000. I've almost gotten over that."

Football, of course, has never gotten over Johnny Blood.

At Notre Dame coaches had suggested Blood go out for tackle in spite of his slender physique. He declined, saying the tackle's business was to make contact while his football philosophy was to avoid it. That is perhaps the major difference between ball carriers in the sport: whether you run around people or through them.

The Chicago Bears of the 1930s earned the nickname "Monsters of the Midway" because of the size of their players. Two of the Bears' fairest flowers, Bronko Nagurski and "Jumbo" Joe Stydahar, shown here in action, personified the pro players of those days—"40 or 50 pounds heavier than in college and 200 percent meaner."

Until the advent of Jim Brown, the man against whom all other power runners were measured was Bronko Nagurski, a six-two, 230-pound terror from northern Minnesota with a 19-inch neck and an inborn certainty that the shortest distance between two points is a straight line.

Coach Steve Owen of the New York Giants suggested the only way to stop Nagurski was to "shoot him before he leaves the clubhouse." Mel Hein said, "The first tackler slows him down. The second spills him. The third pins him on the ground. The system is not foolproof. We lost a lot of players that way."

From 1932 until 1938 and again during a 1943 comeback,
Nagurski rampaging downfield with a hapless defender hanging
on for the ride and others scattered about like chips of wood was
perhaps the single most common sight in the NFL. The myths
about his awesome power die hard. There was the day he ripped
off center, dropped two linebackers, belted a defensive halfback
and crashed over safely for a touchdown before running headfirst
into the wall behind the end zone. Returning to the huddle, he
said, "That last guy hit me awfully hard."

There is even the story that a scout discovered him plowing a
field outside his International Falls home near the Canadian border. When the scout asked him for directions, Nagurski picked
up the plow and pointed—and he was on his way to Minnesota. There he established the image of Coach Bernie Bierman's
Northmen running amok through the country's stadia during the
1930s. A university physiologist found him "the most perfectly
coordinated human being I've ever seen."

He was an All-American tackle. In his senior year squad needs
moved him at fullback and he made All-American ranking on at
least one chart there. It was not only his size, impressive for the
day, that contributed to his legend; there was also his prodigious
strength. He liked to enter rooms with his wife held in the palm
of his hand.

He was more than a power runner. In 1934 Chicago's Beattie
Feathers set a record for the time by gaining 1,004 yards for the
season. The smallish Feathers picked up most of it by running
behind Nagurski, his hand on the small of the Bronko's back—a
tug escorted by a liner.

We have already seen how Nagurski won the first title game
against New York in 1933. The key play sent Nagurski powering
toward the line only to stop short, straighten up and pass over
the heads of defenders massed to stop him. It worked for two
touchdowns in that contest and was a consistent factor in the
Bear attack through Nagurski's career. And even though the
Giants avenged themselves 30-13 in the sneakers game the following year, two touchdowns by Nagurski were called back in
the first half.

The feint into the line followed by the pass was unveiled

against Portsmouth at the end of the 1932 season. The two teams had finished even and, this being before the playoffs were instituted, met to settle the issue of which was best. Freezing weather gripped the city so completely that officials decided to move the game indoors to Chicago Stadium. It was a less formal era.

But even playing on an 80-yard field the teams were deadlocked near the end of the fourth quarter. Then Chicago, led by Nagurski, powered to the Spartan one-yard line. The Bronko, as everyone figured, rammed into the line. But three times a concentrated Portsmouth defense stopped him.

On fourth down he stepped toward the line and then, as defenders congregated, lofted the ball to Grange in the end zone for the game's winning touchdown. Portsmouth Coach George "Potsy" Clark protested that he was not five yards behind the line of scrimmage as the rules of the day provided on a pass play. The officials' decision, as it usually does, stood up.

But at the next league meeting, George Preston Marshall, using the dispute as an example, pressed successfully for a rule change that permitted passing from anywhere behind the line of scrimmage. It opened up the sport and led to the development of the game as it is played today.

Nagurski picked up almost 8,000 yards during his first eight seasons, most of them against defenders concentrating on stopping him. His average carry was 4.6 yards. Off the field he developed a highly successful professional wrestling career. When the years had slowed him, he devoted all his time to wrestling with no major loss of income. He never made more than $5,000 a season playing football.

"For the times," he said, "I got good money. It was all I could ask for. Football doesn't owe me a living." It is hard to imagine the league's outstanding player saying any such thing today.

But Nagurski wasn't through. Six years after his retirement the Bears asked him to come back to bolster up a squad weakened, like all teams, by the loss of members serving in World War II. He played at tackle. In the season's finale against the Cardinals, the Bears trailed 24-14 in the third quarter. And then as the crowd thrilled to the change, Nagurski moved to fullback. It was a sight out of old as he powered the team down the field, banging away at the center of the line in short bursts all the way to the goal. The Bears won that game 32-24, and it remained Nagurski's greatest thrill.

It wasn't the only time he turned a game around. Early in his career his defensive lapse allowed Portsmouth to take a 14-10 lead. On the verge of tears, he asked for the ball after the following kickoff. He went 55 yards for a score—ignoring six attempted tackles—to win the game.

He continued wrestling until he was nearly 60 before settling in for good in his beloved north country on the shores of Rainy Lake at the Canadian border. One of his sons, Bronko, Jr., was a 250-pound All-American tackle at Notre Dame and later a star in the Canadian League. Another son weighed 205 pounds as a high school freshman.

But if they were bigger, none could erase the picture of the old man storming toward the goal line like Paul Bunyan on the loose. Once, Hall of Famer Dutch Clark made only a half-hearted attempt at tackling the touchdown-bound Nagurski in the clear. His coach was asked if he bawled out Clark. "Hell, no," he said. "I wouldn't have tried to stop the son of a gun either. Besides, it wouldn't have done any good."

Other Hall of Fame backs—Van Buren, Marion Motley—poked away at Nagurski's records, but he remained the power back to measure all others by. And then along came Brown.

No one who ever saw Jim Brown run on a football field could forget him. His approach to the line seemed almost thoughtful, almost slow, and he slipped through imaginary openings like a man picking his way through a mine field. He was the explosion, running straight up—not like Nagurski or the other crouching, crushing runners of old—sweeping elegantly into the clear; six feet, two inches, 230 pounds, running with a kind of elegant grace.

Brown said, "I don't go into the line in the traditional fullback manner. You don't find me leading with my head. Most of the time the only contact is my shoulder pads. Normally I start with small steps so I'll be able to turn or slide toward the opening. When the tackler comes at me I drop the shoulder. The runner's shoulder should be the first thing to hit the tackle."

The picture of grace, almost daintiness, was deceptive. Said

Anyone who saw Jim Brown play knew he was the greatest runner of all. He ran for more than 12,000 career yards and 127 touchdowns.

Ed O'Bradovich, the hard-bitten defensive end of the Chicago Bears, "When I was a rookie I hit him solidly at the line of scrimmage on first down. When I got up I said to myself, "That Jim Brown isn't so great." Then I heard the field announcer say it was second down and two feet to go."

Bill Pellington, a rugged linebacker for the Baltimore Colts, frequently was asked who was the hardest man to bring down in the NFL. After he ran through his personal list, the point would be made that he hadn't mentioned Jim Brown. "I can't," said Pellington. "I never brought him down."

As a rookie Brown gained an incredible 982 yards. He bettered that mark in each of the nine years he played. Only 11 men had gained 1,000 or more yards a season in NFL history. Brown did it seven times. He led the league in rushing eight of his nine years. When he gained 1,863 yards in 1963 he became the first man ever to run for more than a mile in a single season. His career total of 12,312 yards, never even approached by any other runner, was just eight yards short of seven miles. He scored 127 touchdowns.

With a perfectly molded 45-inch chest tapering to a 32-inch waist, it is small wonder that he was once introduced at a banquet: "Gentlemen, I give you Superman."

Brown was born on St. Simon's Island, Georgia, in 1936. His parents separated when he was two and he came north with his mother. They settled in Great Neck, Long Island, outside New York City. He was big early, an acknowledged leader among his fellows. He was head of a teenage gang but soon channeled his energies in sport, breaking all the schoolboy football records on the Island. As a 200-pound senior, he averaged almost 15 yards a carry and, in basketball, set a local record with a 55-point display.

It was not an easy early life. His mother, who worked as a domestic, sent him to school in Manhasset by taxi, a big expense on a limited budget. Later he boarded with a black family until she found an apartment for them. She saw to it, however, that he was well clothed and taken care of.

Some 45 colleges expressed an interest in him after he finished ravaging the record books. Syracuse was not among them, but an alumnus of that college made it possible for him to attend without an athletic scholarship. He was the only black on the team, a surprising circumstance in light of the black stars that followed his steps to the school—Ernie Davis, Jim Nance, Floyd Little, among them.

He became, of course, the greatest athlete in the school's history, starring in basketball and track as well as football. He also achieved All-American rating in lacrosse, a sport in which he was even better than he is in football, which stretches the imagination. He picked up 986 yards his senior year, capping it by scoring 43 points against Colgate. A pass interception, three fumbles and a blocked point-after touchdown cost Syracuse the Cotton Bowl game against Texas Christian, 28-27. But Brown put forth the most awesome display of power football ever seen in the Dallas stadium. He scored 21 points, often carrying several foes on his back as he ran for 132 yards in 26 carries.

The jury wasn't out long after he arrived in Cleveland. "The best draft choice we ever made," said Paul Brown. He picked up 89 yards in his professional debut against the Giants. Facing a third and 11 late in the game, Cleveland was expected to pass. Instead, Brown burst up the middle for 15 yards, setting up a Lou Groza field goal that won the game 6-3.

But it was against Los Angeles that rookie year that Brown put on the greatest single running exhibition in league history. After the Browns blew a 14-point lead to Van Brocklin and his cohorts, Brown fumbled and the Rams went ahead 28-17. Brown, angry at himself, responded by scoring four touchdowns, setting a league record he subsequently tied by running for 247 yards in a single game.

Against Philadelphia his longest single gain in 31 carries was "only" 18 yards, but it was a typical Brown maneuver. The play was a sweep to the right. He was hit behind the line of scrimmage and again just beyond it, but he kept moving to the three-yard line. He scored four times that day. "You hear all about second effort," said one onlooker. "He gives fourth effort."

The reign of terror had begun. A Washington tackle tried to clothesline Brown, that is, hurt him with an extended arm at chin level. "He almost tore my arm off," reflected the tackle. His jousts with New York's Sam Huff were historic. The Giants enjoyed some successful days against Cleveland, with Huff assigned to be Brown's policeman. But Huff said, "All you can do is grab him, hang on and wait for help." He made the mistake of telling Brown, "Hey, Jim, you stink," after stopping him a few times. Brown responded with a 65-yard touchdown run, calling back from the end zone, "Hey, Sam. How do I smell from here?"

The Giant defense was the strongest in the league those years. It enjoyed its proudest moments when it stopped Brown. But there were days like this: Brown opened the proceedings taking a flare pass for 30 yards. He scored from the three-yard line, cut-

ting back so suddenly defenders were twisted helplessly as he
strolled into the end zone; he scored from four yards out, running
straight over the safety man; he scored from the 27, finding an
imaginary hole, breaking tackles, being hit at the six by two men,
dragging them to the three and falling forward for his third score
of the day, gaining 156 yards in 20 carries, as Cleveland won
43-21. Giant Coach Allie Sherman said, "Four yards of pop will
keep you in any running game, and, hell, he falls down for four
yards."

But Brown said, "Yardage isn't the big thing. Winning the
championship is. That's what I work for. Winning the championship." And in 1964 the Browns did just that, defeating the Giants
for the conference crown on the final day of the season 54-20
as Brown gained 99 yards.

It was a time when the West was rated the superior division.
At least three teams in that conference were figured tougher than
anything the East could offer, and Baltimore was a resounding
choice to handle the Browns. Cleveland won one of the sport's
great upsets, 27-0, as Brown carried for 114 yards.

Even in that championship season Brown had his critics. He
was totally his own man off the field—autocratic some said. He
led a players' revolt in 1962, charging Paul Brown was out of
touch. "Either Paul Brown goes, or I do," he said. Owner Art
Modell responded to the ultimatum by firing the coach, but the
controversy reflected on the player, although he later said, "Paul
Brown inserted me right away as a rookie even though I hadn't
played much in the All-Star game. That developed my confidence. He believed in me."

To critics who questioned his blocking he answered, "I get
paid for running, not blocking. . . . If I had another guy who was
doing the running, I'd be the best blocker in the league."

On the field no way was found to stop him. Suggested De-
troit's Alex Karras: "Give each guy on the line an ax." He was
indestructible, never injured, and he didn't smoke or drink.
Meanwhile, Brown, a handsome man, took on a movie career.
When rains delayed production of a picture in 1965, Modell said
Brown would be fined for every day that he missed in camp.
Brown retired. The team had just won a championship and he
was near the height of his power but he resisted dictation.

Some questioned the decision. Actor Lee Marvin jokingly said Brown "is a better actor than Olivier would be a football player," but the movie career was a success. Soon Brown was making more money for a single movie than he did in a season as one of the game's highest paid players. He became a moving force in the Black Economic Union, an organization "providing capital and opportunity for blacks to advance themselves within the system."

And as soon as the mandatory waiting period of five years after retirement passed, Brown was named to the Hall of Fame. He said, "My mother had a hard time when I was growing up. I have never told her so before now, so I thought I would take the opportunity now to say how grateful I am. . . . The arrogant, bad Jim Brown can give true love when he is with people he knows and can respect."

10 / THE BACKS COME CHARGING BY

If Brown with his combination of great power and deceptive speed, remains a towering figure among running backs, the Hall is peopled with men whose dedication to the great game revealed itself in a kind of ceaseless devotion to the goal line.

There is George McAfee, Sid Luckman's favorite, whose water bug maneuvers so often broke things open for the Bears; and there is Cliff Battles, the Phi Beta Kappa from West Virginia Wesleyan whose six-year career ended in a minor salary dispute with George Preston Marshall. Rather than play for less than he thought he was worth, Battles gave up the game for a career as a business executive.

He was three times an All-Pro, including 1933 when he led the league with 874 yards rushing. Against the Giants in the playoffs he put together runs of 71, 78 and 55 yards. "He had the knack of following blockers better than any ball player I've seen," said Sammy Baugh. In the Redskins' championship year of 1937, Battles gained 164 yards in a 49-14 rout of the Giants. The total didn't include a 75-yard dash with an intercepted pass.

As Battles served to keep the pressure off Baugh, Marion Motley kept the backfield a safe place to play for Otto Graham. Motley's statistics are impressive enough—4,620 yards in nine pro seasons—but they do not reflect his services as perhaps the best blocking back of the power runners. He was enormously strong, capable of sending would-be tacklers flying like bowling pins, but he was also quick. Said Paul Brown, "He was as fast a big man as there is in sport. . . . His type of ball carrying is the kind of thing in which we trap linemen to keep them from rushing Graham. . . . They don't want Motley in their secondary because the smaller men who might have to tackle him will get hurt."

Motley's association with Brown went back a long way. The two men remembered each other from the days when Brown was compiling an amazing coaching record at Ohio's Massillon High School and Motley played for the rival Canton McKinley team. Brown moved on to Ohio State and then to the Great Lakes Naval Training Academy. Motley played for the University of Nevada before joining the service. He called Brown and was quickly assigned to the team which was good enough to roll over Notre Dame 39-7.

After the war, when Brown was organizing the Cleveland Browns, there was one black man on the squad, guard Bill Willis of Ohio State. Motley received his chance largely because the team needed a roommate for Willis, so touchy were those days. The bonus, of course, is that both men became immediate stars.

"Just run right after them and over them," Brown advised the 230-pound back with sprinter's speed. Motley put the advice to the test in an early game with the Chicago Rockets. Elroy Hirsch was the man he met head-on. Motley was off for a long touchdown and the Browns to a 20-7 victory.

It was a time when a black player was a rarity in professional football. A rival owner attending the game with the late Vic Morabito who owned the San Francisco 49ers, asked him why he had signed rusher Joe Perry. A moment later, Perry flashed for a 63-yard touchdown. "Any questions?" asked Morabito.

Perry teamed with Hugh McElhenny to give the 49ers a unique distinction—the only team with a set of running backs destined for the Hall of Fame. He came to San Francisco in 1948 from Compton Junior College. Frankie Albert, handing off to him said. "That guy takes off like a jet." It was Joe "the Jet" after that. He went 47 yards for a touchdown the first time he handled

139 THE BACKS COME CHARGING BY

the ball in the AAFC.

The records he set shattered Van Buren's and lasted until Brown came along—8,280 yards in 13 seasons. That's a long time for a running back. "If I get hurt," he said, "John just tells me that's the breaks of the game." John was his 13-year-old son.

The Jet was the first man to gain more than 1,000 yards rushing in two consecutive seasons. A typical performance came against the Bears in 1953. San Francisco trailed until the Jet shifted into high gear. The final score was 35-28, Perry scoring three times. McElhenny embellished the performance with 52 yards on two kickoff returns, 32 on two punt returns and 50 yards on sweeps. When San Francisco overcame three George Blanda touchdown passes to defeat the Bears 31-24 the following year, Perry's 53-yard run set up a seven-yard touchdown for McElhenny. Three minutes later he went 58 yeards, setting up a fullback plunge for John Henry Johnson. Perry gained 119 yards that day, McElhenny 114.

Like Perry, McElhenny lasted 13 years in the NFL. The first nine were with the 49ers before he made appearances with Minnesota and New York. He was injured so much of the time that it reduced his effectiveness, but his 5,281 yards rushing stood for a time as second best on the NFL career list.

It is surprising he played at all. When he was 11 he stepped on a broken milk bottle, severing all the tendons in his foot. One doctor said it was doubtful that he would walk again. He spent five months in bed.

But he came out of it the specialist in the dazzling long run that earned him the nickname of "the King." It was a career pursuit for him, symbolized by a 105-yard kickoff return at Compton, a 100-yard punt return at the University of Washington and a 94-yard punt-return touchdown with the 49ers.

Huff said, "He gave me a heart attack every time he had the ball." Van Brocklin said, "He was the greatest runner I ever saw. The King was over the hill at the time, but I'll never forget a run against the 49ers. It was only 39 yards, but nine men had shots at him. None could hold him."

"I try not to run into people," said this artful dodger, master of the sidestep and pirouette, the spin and the burst of speed. "I try to hit a piece of the tackler."

Hugh McElhenny, "the King," teamed with Joe "the Jet" Perry to give San Francisco a ground force roughly equivalent to an earthquake. His moves were so effective that at times defenders fell down without touching him.

When his glory days were behind him, McElhenny scored the key touchdown for New York on a little flare pass against the Browns. His moves were so effective that two defenders fell down without touching him.

But perhaps his greatest service was saving the San Francisco franchise. It was on shakey pinnings when he joined the club in 1952, but the crowds turned out to delight at a rookie who put together an astonishing 10.69 average rushing, receiving, returning punts and kickoffs and running with interceptions. It stood as the second best in NFL history.

The 49ers trailed the Colts 13-10 in 1957 with McElhenny then at end, which he said "is like being a spectator." Tittle was injured and a jittery John Brodie took over. "Throw the ball to me," McElhenny suggested. "I can beat my man in the end zone." Brodie got it there and the 49ers won 17-13.

He had been the most sought-after schoolboy in the country after setting hurdle records as a Los Angeles trackman. But a high mark for going after an athlete was set by Charles Bidwill, owner of the Chicago Cardinals, who paid Charley Trippi the then unheard of bonus of $100,000 to sign. Bidwill died before he could see his dream backfield play, but Trippi, Christman, Elmer Angsman and Harder won the championship in 1947 defeating the Eagles of Van Buren 28-21. Trippi scored on a 44-yard run from scrimmage and a 75-yard punt return.

Trippi was the definitive all-everything as a collegian, a serviceman and a pro. No less than Thorpe called him "the greatest football player I've ever seen. He's an excellent runner, passer and blocker, a great punter and tackler. I guess that covers the field."

So did Trippi who came out of Pittstown, Pennsylvania High School to lead the University of Georgia freshmen to an undefeated season. When he moved on to the varsity there was another Pennsylvania rebel there, Frankie Sinkwich, also an All-American. So Coach Wally Butts moved Sinkwich to fullback in midseason. The two engineered a 9-0 upset of UCLA in the Rose Bowl, Trippi rushing the ball to the two-yard line. Sinkwich, in spite of two sprained ankles, took it in from there.

Trippi's college career was interrupted for two years with the Air Force, during which time he made the All-Service team. But he came back to spark a 20-6 win over Tulsa in the Oil Bowl with a 68-yard punt return. He led the 1947 team to an undefeated season, winning the Maxwell Award and All-American rating with 14 touchdowns, 744 yards on the ground, 622 yards passing. After the team defeated the University of North Carolina with its All-American Charley "Choo Choo" Justice, 20-10, Butts singled out Trippi's defensive contributions in addition to his 67-yard touchdown pass. "He's the greatest safety man I've coached," he said. "Consistently great." Georgia Tech's Bobby

Charley Trippi was an All-American at the University of Georgia when he joined the Chicago Cardinals to form the sport's first dream backfield. A rival coach in college confessed, "There's no way of stopping him." While the pros proved that wasn't literally true, Trippi played up to the spirit of the comment.

Dodds called Trippi, "The greatest I ever saw. There's no way of stopping him."

If there was, NFL teams didn't apply it very successfully. Trippi set a club rushing mark of 3,511 yards over nine seasons for a 5.7 average.

It was the final flush of the all-purpose back, and if any other measured up to Trippi it was the Hall of Famer called "Bullet" Bill Dudley, who played at 175 pounds and was so small that in spite of an illustrious high school career in his native Virginia attracted no scholarship offers except from the state university.

"That was only because I could place-kick," he explained.

As it turned out, he could do anything on the field, making All-Pro as a rookie with the Pittsburgh Steelers. Sixteen when he played his first college game, he was an All-American at 19. He led the league in rushing in 1942 and 1946 and set a club record with ten pass interceptions.

But he could not get along with Coach Jock Sutherland, stubborn exponent of the single wing. The tailback position exposed Dudley to constant punishment. He was not particularly fast, relying on change of pace and guile to work his wonders, and he said, "I'm not big enough to take such a beating." He was traded to Detroit at his own request and wound up with Washington as a place-kicker. He did more than boot the ball. Once he kicked off four times in a game, four times making the tackle. The fifth time he threw a blocker into the receiver. The sixth time he recovered a fumble.

If the shifting fortunes of football put emphasis on the specialist on offense rather than the triple threat in the Trippi-Dudley mold, it also made room for the back who didn't play offense at all. To the casual fan, the man with the ball is the king. To the insider, it's a matter of relative importance. Van Brocklin, one of the greatest quarterbacks, said that blockers make the quarterback. More surprisingly he also said, "I'd rather play quarterback and linebacker or cornerback. Why? Those are harder positions to play. The linebacker has to think. His position is position." And he said of Jack Christiansen, "He was the best defensive back I ever played, a sort of football center fielder of the Willie Mays type." McElhenny recalls that Christiansen three times took touchdowns away from him. The defensive unit Christiansen headed with Detroit from 1951 to 1958 was the best in the game. "Chris' Crew" it was called, featuring Bill Stits, Jim David and Carl Karilivacz, beside Christiansen. As much as the Bobby Layne offense it put Detroit into the playoffs four times, winning three championships.

A graduate of Colorado State University—Colorado A & M at the time—Christiansen went on to make All-Pro six straight times and play in five pro bowls. The honor wasn't strictly for his defensive work—he was also a fearsome kick returner. Eight times he returned punts for touchdowns—a record—on two occasions

Jack Christiansen was captain of "Chris' Crew," the defensive counterpart of Bobby Layne's offense in the early 1950s when Detroit and Cleveland traditionally battled it out for the championship. His return of eight punts for touchdowns set a league record.

returning the kick twice in a game. In 1951 he averaged better than 21 yards returning punts—another record—and his career average of 12.75 is second to McAfee's. The tenacity of his defensive play was reflected in his coaching when he took over the San Francisco 49ers where he put together a simplified offense. The squad lost ten in a row, including pre-season games, before it upset unbeaten Chicago. The game ball, which could have gone to any of the players, was presented to Christiansen "because he had the guts to stick with the offense until it worked."

It's axiomatic now that the best athlete will be tested as a defensive back. It wasn't always that way. Emlen Tunnell came to the Giants in 1948 from the University of Iowa where he'd been an outstanding halfback. The first black to play for New York, he was juggled uncertainly from offense to defense. After a disastrous game against Washington he was called to account by Coach Steve Owen. "Wasn't that Sammy Baugh the greatest passer you ever saw?" "Yes, sir," said Tunnell. "Well, it will cost you $100. The next time you want to watch the game, buy a ticket," said the coach.

Tunnell became a little more active after that. But it wasn't until his third year that he learned the joys of defense. Owen installed what was called "the umbrella defense," so-called because the alignment of the defensive backfield resembled an open umbrella. It was designed specifically to blunt the passing of Otto Graham and the running of Marion Motley. It worked. New York pinned the first shutout ever on the Browns.

"That was the best tackling backfield I ever saw," said Tunnell. "After the first Cleveland game I really never wanted to play offense again." In 14 NFL seasons he never did. He set records with most interceptions—79, and most yards returned with interceptions—1,282, as well as a lifetime total of 258 punts returned. Four times an All-Pro, perhaps his most remarkable distinction came in 1952 when he rolled up 924 yards gained as a defensive back. The offensive leader that year was Deacon Dan Towler of the Los Angeles Rams with 894 yards—the only time a defensive back outgained an offensive player over a year.

Perhaps the highest praise that can be given players like Tunnell and Christiansen is to call them coaches on the field. But the ultimate responsibility for shaping the team, of course, goes to the front office and the coaches themselves. We have seen their handiwork throughout this book. Owners like Halas and Mara and Art Rooney of Pittsburgh who stayed with the game when it was struggling; coaches like Halas—there he is again!—and Steve Owen of the Giants, whose career dated back to service as a tackle with the old Kansas City Cowboys and lasted through the modern T, but who insisted that "football is a game played down in the dirt, and it always will be. There's no use getting fancy about it."

Greasy Neale too, is in the Hall of Fame, for those championship Eagles teams with an offense that could be outlined on the
back of a brown paper bag. But as professional football crested
into a popularity that saw it named the number one spectator
sport in America, one man symbolized the sport to its fans. He
came out of a hard school and he believed that life is real. But in
a troubled time he took on a significance beyond the field itself.

He was, of course, Vince Lombardi.

11 / THE COACH AND THE GAME

The facts are simple enough. Vince Lombardi took over a disorganized Green Bay team that had won four games in two years. The year was 1958. The next year, their first under Lombardi, the Packers were seven and seven. The year after that, they were conference champions. In eight seasons they won six divisional titles, five NFL championships and the first two Super Bowls. The man from the sidewalks of Brooklyn made a little community in Wisconsin a synonym for excellence.

During the ten years of the 1960s, many things seemed wrong in our national life. A President of the United States was assassinated; then a great civil rights leader; then the President's brother. After a hopeful beginning, relations between the races became cautious and ugly. There were conflicts between older people and the young; a new sense of difference between father and son.

It seemed that only in the field of sports did old values remain the same. And the symbol of all this was Vincent Thomas Lombardi and his Green Bay Packers.

The game they played was only football; a game boys play. But 70 million people watched the first Super Bowl game on television. Green Bay, already accepted for half a decade as the best in the National Football League, played against the Kansas

Vince Lombardi had the envied skill of turning dismal teams into national champions. He had a winning combination of toughness, compassion, hard work and faith.

City Chiefs, newcomers from the upstart American Football League. The Packers didn't figure to have trouble with the Chiefs, and they didn't.

But before the game, Frank Gifford, who starred when Lombardi was offensive coach at New York, put his arm around Lombardi, the most feared and revered man in the sport. Gifford, then a television announcer, talked briefly with the coach. He recalled that he felt the coach trembling. "I think it scared him," said Gifford, "that he was representing a 50-year-old institution against a bunch of upstarts."

The jokes about Lombardi's toughness were spread from player to public. "He treats us all alike," said veteran Henry Jordan. "Like dogs." Or, "When Coach says 'Sit down,' I don't look around to see if there's a chair." Old sayings seemed newly minted when they were attributed to Lombardi: "Winning isn't everything. It's the only thing." "You have to pay the price." "Run to daylight."

No one knew better than Lombardi that the lessons of football couldn't all be applied to society and life at large. But perhaps the sternest of all Lombardi's sayings is generally applicable: "I think that a boy with talent has a moral obligation to fulfill it, and I will not shrink from my own responsibility."

Perhaps it was that spirit, carried out by the Packers, that appealed to the nation at large. Certainly it is something most of his players, who sometimes hated Lombardi for driving them in practice—driving them until they were weary and hurt—came to understand and respect.

It wasn't just a saying with Lombardi either. It was the way he lived. He grew up in New York, the eldest of five children. His father was a stern taskmaster and hot-tempered, characteristics Lombardi inherited.

Vince thought he wanted to enter the priesthood. He decided otherwise, although he remained a deeply religious man, attending Mass every day of his life. He went to Fordham University, majoring in business. There he became a member of the Seven Blocks of Granite. He wasn't an All-American like center Alex Wojciechowicz, but he battled successfully against football players from the best teams in the country, frequently outweighed by 20 or 30 pounds. A teammate remembers Lombardi wasn't the best player, the best student, the most determined character, but he ranked near the top in all those attributes.

Too small for pro ball, and with no idea of coaching, Lombardi put in a couple of years as an insurance investigator. Then he succeeded a Fordham teammate as head football coach at St. Cecilia High School in Englewood, New Jersey. As part of the deal he also had to coach the basketball team. He didn't know much about basketball, but he coached the squad to a state championship. His football teams once ripped off 32 straight wins. This was with a student body of some 500, 250 of them boys.

Lombardi excelled at getting the most from the least. After a tour coaching the Fordham freshmen, he joined the West Point coaching staff under Earl "Red" Blaik, perhaps the greatest college coach of his time. Lombardi later spoke of how much he learned from Blaik. Because of its rigid military requirements, the Academy seldom attracts great athletes. Good ones, but not superstars. Blaik was a master at raising those teams to national championship status. So it was the first year Lombardi worked as an assistant.

There followed some good times. And then disaster struck. A scandal involving cheating on examinations wiped out the football team. It was a serious blow to morale that affected the entire Academy. But two years later, making imaginative use of the material at hand, Army was back at the top again. Lombardi learned perhaps most of all how to organize time. As a professional coach his practices seldom lasted more than the hour or two a day that was the routine at West Point.

He moved to New York as offensive coach of the Giants in 1954. The previous year New York won only three games, scoring 179 points. An All-American halfback from Southern California named Frank Gifford was used largely on defense. Lombardi shifted Gifford to offense, making him a Pro Bowl selection five years in a row. As for the offense as a whole, it never scored fewer than 246 points.

A similar disaster area waited in Green Bay when Lombardi, 45 years old, received his first chance at head coaching in the pros. Rooting around the bottom of the league, operated by a divided board of directors in a cold community in the northland, the Packers seemed far from the glory days of the 1930s under Curly Lambeau, the Notre Dame graduate who organized the team from workers at the meat packing plants.

From the beginning Lombardi took over. He insisted on full powers as both general manager and coach. As Gifford had been wasted at New York, a Notre Dame All-American named Paul Hornung was close to quitting at Green Bay, shifting from fullback to quarterback. "You're my halfback," said Lombardi after looking at game films. A seventeenth-round draft choice from Alabama named Bart Starr shared quarterback duties. Under

Lombardi he became one of the best in the league.

The championship seasons are legend: the 1960 loss to Philadelphia that ended with fullback Jim Taylor in the grip of Chuck
Bednarik and the Packers sure they should have won the game;
the following year's rout of the Giants, followed by another defeat of New York; the 22-12 clobbering of Cleveland and a 34-27
win over Dallas.

But perhaps the single most famous game of the decade was
the following year's 21-17 victory over Dallas. Perhaps fittingly,
the most famous play of the decade, determining the outcome,
revolved around a block.

At a time when a lot of nonsense was being spouted in the
nation and reflected in football—talk of new formations and
momentum and mystique—Lombardi liked to argue that football
was a matter of blocking and tackling. "The team that blocks
and tackles better wins. It's as simple as that."

The game pitted the Packers, going for a record third straight
NFL championship, against a younger Cowboy team rated at
least its equal in personnel. It was played at Green Bay in 13
below-zero weather conditions, perhaps the worst ever for a
title game. The Packers hopped off to a 14-0 lead. But Dallas,
defiant of charges that it couldn't win the big ones, came back
to tie the game and then go ahead 17-14. With five minutes left,
the Packers got the ball. They drove down the field—68 yards in
12 plays. With no time outs remaining they had the ball on
the Dallas one.

Starr scored on a quarterback sneak following a block by
Jerry Kramer that almost instantly made Kramer the most
famous offensive lineman in football. In the madhouse that was
the winning Packers' dressing room, Kramer was called before
the television cameras. There had been much written about
Lombardi's toughness, the way he drove players, the way some
feared and hated him. Struggling to make himself heard, Kramer
said:

"There's a great deal of love for one another on this club.
Perhaps we're living in Camelot. Many things have been said
about Coach, and he is not always understood by those who
quote him. The players understand. This is one beautiful man."

"One beautiful man." The rest was anticlimatic. The play—that

game-winning block on the frozen field—seemed to symbolize
the hard requirement of excellence in one line of endeavor at
the time of great national confusion.

The Packer's second Super Bowl victory in a row followed,
as recorded in the Hall of Fame area given over to the Super
Bowls. It reflects the emergence of the American Football
League, the third to bear that name but the first to become
part of a major league sport. There the Joe Namaths and Bob
Grieses mark time until they become eligible for the Hall.

Lombardi stepped down as coach while his team was at the
top. But his restless nature could not resist challenge. He did not
want to become a dead legend in his lifetime. He rather wel-
comed challenge as surely as it met living with defeats.

So he came back as coach and general manager of the Washington Redskins, a team with almost as dismal a record as the
Packers when he took over. He brought them to their first winning season in 14 years.

The following year, stricken with cancer, he died.

But during the greatest decade of the sport's existence he was
its giant. Like others in the Hall of Fame, he represents achievement to those who follow. As a schoolboy, Y. A. Tittle idolized
Sammy Baugh. Joe Namath wasn't even born when the Chicago
Bears, coached by a founder of the NFL, routed Baugh's Redskins. There is a continuity in the game. It is only a step, it
seems, from schoolboy to a place in the Hall. . . . Perhaps it will
happen to the schoolboy who reads this book.